CW00421739

GRAND SLAM!

For my parents

GRAND SLAM!

YEAR OF THE DRAGON

PAUL REES
FOREWORD BY
GERALD DAVIES CBE

MAINSTREAM
PUBLISHING
EDINBURGH AND LONDON

First published in Great Britain in 2005 by
MAINSTREAM PUBLISHING COMPANY
(EDINBURGH) LTD
7 Albany Street
Edinburgh EH1 5UG

ISBN 1 84596 061 0

The match facts appearing in Appendix 2 are reproduced
courtesy of COMPUTACENTER, recorded under guidance
and direction of Stephen P. Smith (WRU referee) who
objectively reports on all decisions made by match officials.

A catalogue record for this book is available from
the British Library

Typeset in Meta and Times

Printed in Great Britain by
Creative Print and Design, Wales

Acknowledgements

A THOUSAND THANKS TO THE FOLLOWING FOR THEIR HELP IN the preparation of this book: David Llewellyn, of *The Independent*, for selflessly giving up his time, compiling the statistics, reading every word and striving valiantly to turn water into wine; Mike Burton, the former Lions, England and Gloucester prop; Ben Clissitt, the sports editor of *The Guardian*, who readily agreed to time off at the shortest of notice; John Connolly, the Bath Rugby head coach; Gerald Davies, the former Lions, Wales and Cardiff wing, a boyhood hero; Alun Donovan, the Wales selection adviser who was out of the game for far too long; Ray Gravell, the former Lions, Wales and Llanelli centre who never lost the faith; Alastair Hignell, the former England full-back; Horace Jefferies, the Cross Keys RFC historian, one of the stalwarts who pumps Welsh rugby's blood; Garin Jenkins, the former Wales and Swansea hooker and a fellow Gooner; John

Scott, the former England and Cardiff captain; Andy Selby, of Computacenter; Professor David Smith, co-author, with Gareth Williams, of one of the indispensable books on rugby union, *Fields of Praise*; Bill Campbell and Ailsa Bathgate at Mainstream Publishing; and, last but certainly not least, my wife, Margaret.

Contents

The Grandest of Slams

5 February 2005 – Wales 11 England 9 (Millennium Stadium)

12 February 2005 – Italy 8 Wales 38 (Stadio Flaminio)

26 February 2005 – France 18 Wales 24 (Stade de France)

13 March 2005 – Scotland 22 Wales 46 (Murrayfield)

19 March 2005 – Wales 32 Ireland 20 (Millennium Stadium)

Foreword

IN 2005, A TOUCH OF GLORY RETURNED TO WALES. ONCE
more, after the long, blighted years of adversity, Welsh rugby
revelled and beguiled on the fields of praise.

Two years after languishing, whitewashed, at the bottom of the
Six Nations Championship without a single victory to their name,
Wales in a remarkable change of fortune were the crowned
champions of Europe for the first time in 11 years. If in 1994 there
was the slight blemish in that they received the championship
trophy at Twickenham on the day they lost to England, there were
no doubts and hesitations at the Millennium Stadium in Cardiff on
19 March 2005. When Martyn Williams, the Welsh flanker who
was later to be named Player of the Tournament, kicked the ball
directly into touch at the West Stand of the National Stadium for
the referee Chris White, of England, to blow the final blast of his
whistle, Wales had conquered all of Europe.

GRAND SLAM!

Wales had won the Grand Slam.

This was the first time in 27 years.

If, in 1978, Wales had accomplished the great deed for the third time in a decade, and, like the sides of 1988 and 1994, had missed it by a shade at least a couple times more, the Grand Slam success of that season was to be recognised as the last for a very long time. The occasional golden moments given us by a few of the single great players of the 1980s and 1990s alleviated only momentarily the poverty which ran through Welsh rugby. Any sense of ambition or pride had deserted Wales's national game.

In the intervening time, Gareth Edwards and I have looked each other in the eye expressing bemusement as the years stretched without reward and the number of empty seasons passed and increased. 'If someone had told us in 1978 that we would not win another Grand Slam in these many years – a quarter of a century? – I would not have believed him' has always been the gist of our thoughts. In both our eyes there lay a melancholy regret and a deep-rooted sadness. Someone somewhere had continually got it wrong for such a long time to pass and to tolerate failure as the inevitable way of our rugby life.

What should have been a source of inspiration to lift Welsh rugby was seen as a millstone to hold it back.

But not so in 2005. The new kids on the block bucked the trend. With insouciance and verve they ran and played throughout the season as if the game was young again. This was rugby with a spring to its step and a smile on its face. Their rugby was unalloyed joy to watch although there were times when all of Wales watched through hand-covered eyes the clock tick down the slow seconds to the game's end.

To start winning again, in whatever shape it took and by whatever margin or means, was a desperate need for Wales. The country had suffered too long. 'To win, to win . . . any old win will do.' But to the 2005 vintage this was not enough. They wanted more. They wanted to go further.

And so it came to pass that they began in Cardiff before embarking for Rome, Paris and Edinburgh to play memorable rugby along the way before returning unvanquished to wear their laurels of victory at home. On a fine sunny spring day and to the strains of '*Cwm Rhondda*' and 'Hymns and Arias', the Welsh team gave their nation that which they had long dreamed.

Rugby is a rough and tumble game. It needs strength and power, force and pressure. A player needs to be tough and vigorous. Circling the field we sometimes find the shade of the bully too. This is the obvious nature of rugby football for all to see.

This is not all. If it were so, it would be the poorer sport. For sure, to a Welshman it is not and cannot forever be. For better or worse, there is a romantic view that lies in a Welshman's heart. There must be beauty too in rugby; of original expression where an individual player leaves his very own signature. There is drama and derring-do; heroic tackles and dancing toes. In the land that legends inhabit, there must be a poetic imagination at work.

This Welsh team played rugby with panache and adventure, courage and nerve. They revitalised and refreshed the Six Nations Championship so that come the end, dare I say, it was not only the Welsh people that wanted to watch Wales play. They were the talk of European rugby. All Europe wanted to see them play.

'Feed me until I want no more' is what the crowd sang and this wonderful Welsh team duly answered. There were unforgettable moments in every game. We look back and there are memories galore. I shall not mention any names. At one stage or another each one of them made a notable and eye-catching intervention either splitting the defence, stopping his opposite man in his tracks or passing with aplomb and style. They played rugby of brilliance.

GRAND SLAM!

The Welsh comeback has been sudden and surprising. And it has been glorious.

As a Welshman I salute them for once more restoring that long-lost pride in Welsh rugby. But there is more. As a man who loves rugby wherever it is played, I salute them for playing the game which was clever and quick-thinking, daring and swift, stubborn and brave. This was rugby young at heart.

Gerald Davies CBE
Wales Grand Slam winner
1971, 1976 and 1978
April 2005

PROLOGUE

Free Men in Paris

Except in dreams, you're never really free.

Warren Zevon

EVERY SUCCESSFUL CAMPAIGN CONTAINS AT LEAST ONE KEY moment, a turning-point which defines the thin line between glory and despair. For Wales in the 2005 Six Nations, there were two, as there had been in the year of their last Grand Slam 27 years before.

In 1978, the England full-back Alastair Hignell had a late penalty chance to clinch a 9–9 draw in Wales's opening match in the then Five Nations at Twickenham, but narrowly failed. In February 2005, with Wales trailing England 9–8 at the end of normal time, they were awarded a penalty close to the right wing, 40 metres from the try-line. With the angle, the kick measured 50 metres, just out of the range of Wales's goal-kicker, Stephen Jones. Gavin Henson, the Neath-Swansea Ospreys' centre who had celebrated his 23rd birthday at the start of the week, asked his captain Gareth Thomas for the ball. Henson had made his debut 32 months before as a 19 year old, but this was his first appearance in the championship. The decision to let him go for goal appeared to be a triumph of hope over expectation, but Henson, showing the assurance and self-belief his teammates were to mine in the coming weeks, knew his moment had come. 'I never had any doubt that it was going to go over,' he said. 'I had been kicking them in practice all week and all I had to do was take my mind back to the training field.' Henson became an instant national hero and the silver-booted player with the golden touch revelled in the attention, driven by destiny.

The story for Wales after 1978 was largely one of decline, at first slow and then accelerated, punctuated by one-off successes in 1988 and 1994. The 1970s, Welsh rugby's third golden era, left a bitter legacy: as Wales rejoined the ranks of the mortals, unfavourable comparisons were made with the heroes of yesteryear and the road to success became littered with the bones of those who became undone at the moment of reckoning. As Wales's outside-half Neil Jenkins wrote in his autobiography, milestones became millstones, but the average age of the 2005 side was less than the number of years which had passed since the last Grand Slam. 'They are not weighed down by any historical baggage,' said the Wales physiotherapist Mark Davies, who was among the new wave of players tried out at the beginning of the 1980s, in the final week of the 2005 championship. 'Most of them would probably not know a 1970s idol if they passed him in the street. I find that strange because my playing career quickly followed the last golden era, but they are concerned only with creating their own history.'

Henson personified new Wales. When the New Zealander Graham Henry arrived to take over as the national coach in the late summer of 1998, two months after South Africa had put 96 points on Wales in Pretoria (they would have made it to three figures had the hooker Naka Drotske not dropped a pass with the line at his mercy), his extensive list of concerns was topped by the fragile mental state of the players at his disposal, allied to technical shortcomings. New Zealand and Wales are the only two countries in the world which can lay claim to rugby union as their national sport, but Henry detected a crucial difference between them: New Zealanders were more concerned with the now than the then, while the Welsh were always looking for the next Barry John, Gareth Edwards or Mervyn Davies, contemptuous of those who did not measure up to the comparisons, gushing about those who did. 'Welsh supporters are like a shower which is either too hot or too cold,' Henry once lamented. 'You either have to get players down from the clouds or pick them up from the floor. There is no perspective.'

It was a problem which tested Henry's successor and compatriot, Steve Hansen. 'I keep telling the players just how good they are but I don't think they believe me,' he said during Wales's ten-match losing run under him in 2002–03. 'They are used to being knocked down by the media and they tend to accept what is written and said about them.' Hansen was pilloried for constantly saying, in response to questions, that performances were more important than results: after Wales played with such a flourish in the 2005 championship, many observers put it down to the fact that Hansen had been succeeded by a Welshman, Mike Ruddock, who had quickly restored traditional values. It was a dewy-eyed, romantic view which did an injustice to both men. One of the most enduring memories of the 2003 World Cup, a tournament which oscillated between walkovers and dour defensive battles, was the flair and derring-do Wales showed against New Zealand and England. 'We scored some cracking tries under Steve, but they tended to be forgotten because we did not win many matches,' said the Wales three-quarter Mark Taylor. 'The turning-point was the game against the All Blacks in the World Cup: it was part by design and part by accident, but we found a way to play using the whole width of the pitch and we have not looked back.'

When Ruddock took over from Hansen in the summer of 2004, he appreciated that he had inherited a squad of players who were ready to make their mark. Wales had been let down in that year's Six Nations by insecure set-pieces, a defect Ruddock quickly remedied. He brought in Clive Griffiths, who had been released by Hansen, as the defence coach and, crucially, left Scott Johnson, the wavy-haired Australian originally hired by Henry, in charge of skills. Johnson turned down the chance to return home and join the Wallabies' coaching staff because he wanted to finish the work started by Hansen. 'We play a lot of touch rugby under Scott, using the whole width of the pitch, rather than the length,' said Taylor. 'He encourages us to look for space and the handling and passing skills of every player have been enhanced. A lot of the stuff we play looks off the cuff, but much of it is down to the hard work we put in in training.'

Henson may not have felt any pressure while lining up his kick against England, but many of his teammates could not bear to watch. It had been nearly four years since Wales had defeated a country of note. They had pushed every one of the top six close in that period – New Zealand, Australia, South Africa, England, France and Ireland – without being able to close the deal. In the latter stages of his reign, as the conditioning work of the New Zealand fitness coach Andrew Hore began to show a marked effect, Hansen and Johnson started to talk up their players. 'The results will come because the players are good enough,' said Hansen at the end of the 2004 championship, shortly before he returned to New Zealand. 'There is no doubt that we are closer to the rest of the pack than we were before. Mike [Ruddock] will take the team to the next stage: at the rate of the improvement they have shown in the last 12 months, they will be a force in next year's Six Nations and I expect a number of Welsh players to be involved with the Lions in New Zealand.' The Wales team manager Alan Phillips, another appointee in the Henry era, was even more prophetic as he prepared to say farewell to Hansen. 'It is only a matter of time before this team achieves success,' he said. 'We are not that far away at all and Mike's inheritance is a strong one.'

Henson embodied the hardening attitude. He played against England as if born for the big stage, dumping the 18-year-old debutant centre Mathew Tait unceremoniously twice in the tackle. An outside-half by preference, Henson had been used by Ruddock at full-back on the 2004 summer tour to Argentina and South Africa. Wales had taken a makeshift squad because of injuries, and he found himself exposed by the Springboks. Whereas players in the past era may have been irreparably damaged by the experience, Henson was driven by a desire to prove himself and by November, when Wales faced South Africa and New Zealand in their four-Test autumn programme, he had been moved to inside-centre to take over the spot vacated by Iestyn Harris, who had returned to rugby league.

Whereas Harris cut an understated figure, blessed with a capacity to create space for others with his awareness and range of passing skills and his ability to ghost past defenders in a manner faintly reminiscent of Barry John, Henson was more assertive and wanted to be a centre of attention. He made no secret of his desire to play at outside-half but, as the All Blacks had done with Daniel Carter, Wales deployed him at inside-centre to give him more time to make decisions and empower him with a broader outlook, making him ready for the day when he would take over the number 10 jersey.

GRAND SLAM!

Harris had had an uncomfortable transition from rugby league to union after joining Cardiff in the summer of 2001, thrust into the international arena at outside-half after playing only two full matches for his club. His prompt elevation was partly a commercial exercise, with the Welsh Rugby Union looking to make a quick return on the £1 million outlay on the player by boosting the gate for his debut match against Argentina, but the ploy backfired on and off the field. It was virtually Henry's final fling: he had returned from the Lions tour that year mortally wounded by attacks on him, some from Welsh players, after an unsuccessful Test series when he had left the midweek team to organise their own training sessions. The team he had taken on a ten-match winning run that started in 1999 with an exhilarating display in Paris, which was as breathless as any of the performances in 2005, needed to be rebuilt and though he had identified some of the potential successors who were later to make their mark, such as Henson, Dwayne Peel, Michael Owen, Duncan Jones, Tom Shanklin and Gareth Cooper, he was mentally shattered and, two months after arriving in Wales to act as Henry's assistant, Hansen found himself in charge.

If Harris had a frailty about him which brought to mind Barry John, it was Henson who had the legendary outside-half's core of steel. Barry John, whose six-year international career was all too brief, looked too fragile for a game which in those days contained numerous exponents of the darker arts, but while he possessed grace and style in abundance, he was motivated by winning and proving himself the best, a characteristic which is an inherent part of Henson's make-up. John may not have relished defending, but he put his body on the line when he had to, such as when he tackled the powerful France number 8 Benoit Dauga in Paris in 1971 and stopped what had appeared to be a certain try to help Wales to their first Grand Slam for 19 years, even if it left him with a reshaped nose. Forgotten in the eulogies which poured out after his premature retirement in 1972 was the criticism he received early in his career. Derided as an outside-half who kicked too much and who lacked judgement, John had to remodel his game after the rule introduced in 1968 which outlawed direct kicks into touch outside a player's 22. Few outside-halfs have been better to watch than John, but he was not interested in pleasing aesthetes: he would do whatever it took to win, be it ending the New Zealand full-back Fergie McCormick's international career by incessantly firing varied kicks at him during the Lions' first Test against the All Blacks at Dunedin in 1971, or dropping four goals for Cardiff in the 12–9 victory over Llanelli in 1970 when his brothers, Clive and Alan, were the opposing flankers.

Henson is driven by the same single-mindedness and, like John, does not indulge in false modesty. 'I should imagine we will be superstars and legends now,' said Henson, the day after helping Wales to win the Grand Slam by defeating Ireland at the Millennium Stadium. While Henry vainly tried to put out the fires of expectation which burned in the country with increasing ferocity as his team went on its ten-match winning run, Ruddock gently fanned the flames after Henson's kick had sunk England, aware that the chronic lack of confidence which Hansen had had to deal with after taking over from Henry had been replaced by a burgeoning collective self-belief. Performances were no longer more important than results: Wales needed a victory over a major country, and as far as the Principality is concerned, there is no more cherished scalp than England's. As the roar which greeted Henson's kick still echoed around the streets adjacent to the Millennium Stadium, Ruddock quietly slipped his dogs off the leash and while the opening game, Shane Williams's try excepted, had been a tense, largely dour affair, the next four matches saw the frustrations of the previous quarter of a century explode in a flame of colour as Wales painted Rome, Paris, Edinburgh and Cardiff red.

One kick made all the difference, as it would have 27 years before when Hignell lined up his 40-metre effort in the dying minutes at Twickenham with his side three points behind. The strike rate of modern-day goal-kickers is appreciably higher than it was in the days of amateurism: not only are pitches generally firmer with players using tees rather than digging their own mounds, balls are no longer absorbent and kickers spend countless hours on the training field. 'Even in the 1970s, selectors would generally choose a side and then decide who would take the kicks,' said Hignell, now a BBC reporter. 'You felt the pressure as much then as kickers do now, but in those days you hardly practised and no one bothered about the mental side when it came to preparation. When I took the final penalty against Wales in 1978, having missed with my three previous attempts, I thought the ball was going over. At the last moment, it drifted to the left and passed just wide of the posts. I put my hands to my face and the image was captured by a photographer. Sport is all about small margins: had the ball held its course that day, rugby history would have been different, just as it would if Henson's kick had fallen just under England's bar. 'If' may only contain two letters but it is one of the biggest words in the English language.

'I often recount the moment in after-dinner speeches. I maintain I was responsible for three Grand Slams: France won it in 1977 after I failed with five penalties and they beat us 4–3; I missed four against Wales the following year and when I retired in 1980 England achieved the clean sweep. Goal-kicking is a solitary pursuit and you have to back yourself. I can remember feeling when I took that final attempt against Wales that all eyes were on me and that I not only had the chance to save the match but to give us an opportunity to win it if there was enough stoppage time. Wales were the team to beat in those days, but we had stopped them scoring a try and our forwards had got stuck into them. It just needed one more kick.'

The other pivotal moment in both years came during Wales's third match. In 1978, they found themselves in Dublin, well fancied to beat an Ireland side which had lost seven of its previous eight internationals. Wales were chasing a then unprecedented third consecutive Triple Crown, something they appeared to have achieved when they breezed into a 13–3 lead after 20 minutes. Ireland then fought back to 13–13. 'Their tails were up and our dreams of that triple Triple Crown were fading fast,' recalled Gerald Davies. 'It is at those precise moments that a team needs to play with more than just the heart, with more than just passion. You can come out of the dressing-room feeling such inspiration but halfway through the second half it is very difficult to sum up the right emotions. At those moments, you need to play with skill and with a cool head. It needs courage, of course, but it must be allied with tactical nous.' Wales needed all their reserves of energy and determination to conjure the winning try for the wing J.J. Williams in the final ten minutes, and were too exhausted afterwards to celebrate the victory and their unique achievement.

'Probably no Grand Slam team has received, in the course of the season, more criticism of its jaded play although it was able, consistently, and in the heat of battle, to raise its game at forward and behind,' wrote David Smith and Gareth Williams in *Fields of Praise*, the official history of the WRU. 'They were fully aware, even if a rather blasé public [was] not, of their coach's instructions to enjoy themselves with as much spontaneity as circumstances would allow. The pride of this team demanded that it play this way but not, ever, only to entertain. It played tight when it needed, it danced out of reach when it was required, and it had that someone in its ranks with that answer to whichever question was posed.'

Neither was the 2005 side reliant on one or two players. When BBC viewers voted for the flanker Martyn Williams as their man of the Six Nations, by an overwhelming majority from the runner-up, the Ireland captain Brian O'Driscoll, their abiding impression would have been of the first ten minutes of the second half at the Stade de France. Wales had trailed 15–6 at the interval having been comprehensively outplayed. Both teams had started the Six Nations with two victories, but whereas Wales's successes had been received rapturously by a public which had last celebrated back-to-back opening victories in the championship in 1994, the France coach Bernard Laporte was under fire for boring the pants off French supporters whose anger was barely assuaged by a rare success at Twickenham.

France's only try in nearly three hours had come from a late charge down against Scotland and they rang the changes despite beating England. Wales, whose defence had been an understated feature of their victories against England and Italy, conceded two tries in the opening 12 minutes as France started at a furious pace. Wales's scrum creaked under relentless pressure and the lineout offered little more in the way of succour. Only at the breakdown, where France gave away a number of penalties in promising positions, did Wales enjoy any relief. One more try would surely have sealed it for the French who launched wave after wave of attacks, but it was Wales who had the final score of the half, Stephen Jones kicking his second penalty to leave a scintilla of hope even if the cause looked hopeless to everyone outside the Wales camp, except for an England supporter watching the match in Dublin who took the chance to invest £100 in Wales during the interval at odds of 15–1.

Ruddock, contrary to popular perception afterwards, hardly spoke during the interval. 'I did not tell them anything because they had stared down the barrel of a gun before,' he said. The second row Brent Cockbain remembers a steely calm. 'We relaxed and spoke quietly about things which needed improving,' he said. 'We had been outplayed, hanging on the ropes at times, but only trailed by nine points, which is nothing in the modern game. Winning is a habit and we had rediscovered what it took to succeed. We knew we were not going to dominate the second half as France had the first, and the first ten minutes were going to be hugely important.'

Within ten minutes of the restart, Wales had taken the lead, thanks to Martyn Williams. France had mounted a promising attack in the Welsh 22 when the ball fell loose and into the arms of the outside-half Stephen Jones. Six years before, Wales had stunned France at the start of the game when Neil Jenkins, Jones's predecessor and a stand-off in the same mould, received the ball from the kick off in his own 22 and made a break rather than kicking for touch. It set the tone for a frenetic 40 minutes of rugby and, just as Jenkins had defied his reputation six years before, so on this occasion Jones left defenders clutching at air as he weaved in and out of tackles on an electrifying 50-metre run which finished with Martyn Williams scoring in the corner. It was in that moment that the destiny of the championship was decided.

Williams was winning his 52nd cap, the most experienced forward in the side, but was only playing because of a foot injury suffered by Colin Charvis during Newcastle's Heineken Cup victory over Newport Gwent Dragons three weeks before the start of the Six Nations. Ruddock had left the Cardiff Blues' flanker out of the summer tour, preferring him to spend time in the gym working on his strength and speed. Williams captained Wales five times under Hansen, but in the final stages of the New Zealander's regime found himself on the bench more often than the starting line-up with size counting against him. It seemed perverse that the quickest forward in the squad was consigned to the sidelines at a time when the team was trying to develop a high tempo game, but when given his opportunity against England, a country he had not tasted success against in eight previous attempts, he viewed it as a final chance. 'I had considered whether I had a future in the set-up after being left out of the tour party,' he said. 'Mike was right to give me a rest and I felt reinvigorated at the start of the season.'

It was Williams's sharp-wittedness just minutes after his galvanising first try which took Wales into a lead they were not to lose in Paris as he took a penalty quickly yards from the French line and dived over. 'Wales had ten minutes of the match through Williams and yet they won,' wailed Laporte, but that was only half the story. France, trailing 24–18 in the final ten minutes, laid siege to the Welsh line, kept out by an unyielding defence. Every time an opening looked to have been fashioned, a red jersey would quickly close it.

Wales were hailed at the end of the Six Nations for their attack-minded approach, but their game was two-toned with equal importance placed on defence. Jones and his half-back partner Dwayne Peel may never have missed an opportunity to up the pace of a game – masters of the art of deconstruction, as the French international Thomas Castaignede put it – but just as significant was their work in defence with Jones's first-half tackle on the Ireland wing Girvan Dempsey on the final weekend as equally significant as his break against France.

As with the 1978 vintage, somebody always stood up at decisive moments. 'Two or three years ago, we would not have come back from the first-half onslaught in Paris,' said Martyn Williams. 'Rugby is played a lot in the head and we have so much more self-belief these days. When you have been through the bad times, as we have, you appreciate success all the more but it did not happen overnight. Graham Henry laid a foundation and Steve Hansen built on it. Mike Ruddock saw that he did not need to take it all down.'

While Wales's free-flowing style sometimes appeared to be rugby union's equivalent of the Harlem Globetrotters with the players having a licence to thrill, the freedom was not absolute. What appeared to be off the cuff was often in fact a rehearsed move, but it was the uplifting feeling Wales inspired after years of dominant defences which made their 2005 success so popular, if not universal.

On a flight back to Bristol from Dublin in March after Ireland had beaten England to maintain their 100 per cent record and inflict a third defeat on their opponents the day after Wales had prevailed in Paris, a Bristolian turned to the Irishman next to him and said: 'I hope you go on and win the Grand Slam. The whole of England will be behind you because we cannot stand the Welsh.' He was taken aback by the reply. 'After all the years of misery they have endured, no one should begrudge Wales some success. And besides, any true lover of rugby can only admire the way they are playing. Theirs is the beautiful game.'

CHAPTER 1

On the Road to Find Out

Sometimes I think it's a sin when I feel like
I'm winning when I'm losing again.

Gordon Lightfoot

WALES'S GRAND SLAM IN 1978 WAS THEIR THIRD IN SEVEN
years, and as the Welsh Rugby Union started planning lavish
celebrations to mark its centenary in 1980–81, few foresaw the
gradual but marked decline which was to follow. Wales narrowly
missed out on a clean sweep in 1979, losing to France in Paris by
a point, and they began the new decade by establishing another
record: when they defeated France 18–9 at the Arms Park in
January 1980, it was their 23rd consecutive victory at home in the
Five Nations, eclipsing the landmark established by Wales during
their first golden era in the early 1900s. By March 1982, the tally
had risen to 27 before Scotland, whose previous away victory in
the championship had come six years before to the day, won by a
crushing margin, 34–18, and became the first visiting team to
score five tries at the ground. Not since 1937 had Wales lost to the

other three home unions in the same season and, remarkably, Wales would now have to wait until 1994 to win both their home matches in a Five Nations campaign.

The class of 1978 quickly dissolved. The half-backs, Gareth Edwards and Phil Bennett, retired after the Grand Slam decider against France, followed, after the summer tour to Australia, by Gerald Davies. The flanker Terry Cobner never played in another championship match, while Tony (Charlie) Faulkner and Bobby Windsor, two members of the Pontypool front row, the wing J.J. Williams and the number 8 Derek Quinnell only had one more campaign left in them. Whereas at the beginning of the golden era Wales had been able to absorb the loss of leading players to retirement or rugby league, such as Barry John, Maurice Richards, John Dawes, Glyn Shaw, Delme Thomas, the wing John Bevan, Dai Morris and John Taylor, holes started to appear. Continuity of selection was a key feature of the 1970s when 69 players were capped; that figure was reached in the following decade by the beginning of 1986, something which could not be put down to an explosion of fixtures.

One person foresaw the meltdown, but his warnings were ignored by the WRU, even when New Zealand started the centenary off on the wrong note by romping to a 23–3 victory in Cardiff in November 1980, Wales's biggest loss at home for 98 years. Carwyn James, the coach who had masterminded the Lions' first, and so far only, Test series victory in New Zealand, in 1971, had become a prophet without honour in his own land and his influence was confined to television and a column in *The Guardian*. Only Llanelli and the Lions were to benefit from the vision of James, a Wales outside-half in the 1950s who would surely have won more than two caps had his career not overlapped Cliff Morgan's. The WRU, interviewing him for the position of national coach in the 1970s, was horrified when he demanded the abandonment of the five-strong selection committee and insisted that the coach be given the authority to drive the team in the direction of his choice, a concession the Union was forced to make when Wales entered the wilderness years at the end of the 1980s.

'That most elusive of qualities, the natural flair of the intuitive player, is currently so rare that we wonder what we have done,' James wrote in 1983. 'Too often we see players reacting like unthinking robots. Hiding behind moves – moves which are called before the ball emerges from the set-piece and when its quality is, as yet, unknown – is the escape route for the robot. Wales's back play has for some time been a pathetic apology to the cloud of witnesses who have graced the international field for a century; every one of the five nations has lost sight of the beauty of back play. Crowds now clap at the sight of the kick-ahead and are happy to pay for the privilege. I would prefer my fly-halfs and three-quarters not to think in terms of moves but to play off the fly-half. This is what happened with the 1971 Lions: Mike Gibson and John Dawes never called the moves beforehand. They just played off Barry John, and if Barry decided to run the ball they instinctively carried on.'

Twenty-one years on, when Steve Hansen left Wales to rejoin Graham Henry as part of the New Zealand coaching team, there were many who rejoiced at the elevation of Mike Ruddock, a son of the Gwent valleys who had enjoyed considerable success with Swansea and Leinster in his coaching career, believing his appointment would lead to a return of so-called traditional values never mind that they had, as James observed, been eroded long before the arrival of the two New Zealanders. It was as if the locust years of the late 1980s and much of the 1990s had never happened.

The real decline, though, had commenced in 1988, a year after

GRAND SLAM!

Wales had been beaten 49–6 by New Zealand in the semi-final of the inaugural World Cup. Wales went on to defeat 14-man Australia in the play-off, although their contention that they were the third best team in the world needed to be qualified: they were the third in the World Cup, a tournament in which the luck of the draw plays a part. Wales were then coached by Tony Gray, a north Walian and an academic who had won two caps as a flanker at the end of the 1960s. Gray initially struggled to persuade his backs to play with their heads up and live off their wits, as Hansen was to in 2002. His back division was brimful of attacking potential: Robert Jones and Jonathan Davies were the half-backs, Bleddyn Bowen and Mark Ring were two converted fly-halfs in the centre, while Ieuan Evans and Adrian Hadley were contrasting wings: the former had the quick feet of Gerald Davies and deceptive strength while the latter, a taller figure whose languid and laid-back approach masked a steely resolve, was more like Maurice Richards, shimmying with surprising acceleration.

The full-back was Paul Thorburn, a prolific goal-kicker whose touchline conversion of Hadley's try in the final minute against Australia at Rotorua had sealed the World Cup play-off. He had scored 140 points in 15 Tests and was a proven match-winner. At the start of the 1988 Five Nations, Gray and his fellow selectors dropped Thorburn for the opening match against England at Twickenham, preferring Anthony Clement, the Swansea outside-half who had never played at full-back. The *Western Mail*, outraged, canvassed a poll of its readers and demanded the return of Thorburn. Gray was considered to be playing a game of Russian roulette without an empty chamber by going to Twickenham shorn of a recognised goal-kicker: four of the previous five fixtures between the countries there had been decided by kicks, and though Davies and Ring were to become regular goal-kickers for their clubs, they could not boast a conversion or a penalty between them at international level by the start of 1988, a record which survived the championship.

Gray, in his studious, understated way, had found the key to remove the self-imposed shackles. Hadley scored two tries, the first coming after Clement had fielded a loose kick by the England outside-half Les Cusworth and launched a dazzling counter-attack. Though Ring fluffed all his kicks at goal, by removing the crutch of a dependable goal-kicker Gray had forced his backs to run. Thorburn returned for the injured Clement in the next match, against Scotland at Cardiff, but the fuse had been lit and the result was the most exciting championship match in Cardiff since the 1970s. Scotland, in those days a resourceful side who were themselves to go on and win the Grand Slam two years later, led 20–10 at the start of the second half but a vintage try by Evans, slaloming his way at pace through five defenders, marked the turning of the tide and Wales went to Lansdowne Road seeking their first Triple Crown since 1979. The Irish set out to disrupt Wales's rhythm and unsettle their midfield, succeeding on a windy day where nerves got the better of boldness. It was Thorburn who delivered the 12–9 victory with a penalty in the fourth minute of injury time. Despite his success, however, the wheel had not yet come full circle.

After Wales won the 2005 Grand Slam, their captain, Michael Owen, a 24-year-old number 8 blessed with rare footballing instincts, remarked that the achievement had to be a beginning, not prove to be a one-off. 'Wales won the Triple Crown in 1988 and the Five Nations title in 1994, but they failed to follow them up,' he said. 'We cannot allow that to happen again. The Wales players are the showcase at the top of the structure, but it is not all about us as a team. It is about people buying into the four regions and the academies and making sure that the whole of Welsh rugby is strong. People need to embrace this if this achievement is not to be a one-off.'

GRAND SLAM!

Wales missed out on the Grand Slam in 1988, losing to France by a point in the Cardiff rain despite dominating the first half. Gray was voted the European coach of the year but, flying high in April, he was shot down in June after a tour to New Zealand, the World Cup holders. It was a month which was to expose the soft underbelly of the Welsh game. The opening two provincial matches, against Waikato and Wellington, ended in comprehensive defeats, and though Wales surprisingly beat Otago four days before the first Test, it was clear that they did not have the power or presence at forward to cope with the All Blacks, whose technical superiority was so marked that it was difficult to believe that matches between the countries had been amongst the most eagerly anticipated on the international fixture calendar.

Wales lost the first Test in Christchurch 52–3, their heaviest ever defeat. They leaked ten tries, another record, and the injuries started to pile up. Hadley, like Thorburn, did not go on the tour and the following season he turned to rugby league with Salford; Bowen was ruled out of the tour early on with an injured wrist and his successor as captain, Robert Norster, sustained a knee injury in the first Test which ruled him out for the rest of the trip. The team which lined up for the second Test in Auckland contained just seven of the players who had started against France three months earlier, and Ring was playing out of position at full-back. Jonathan Davies assumed the captaincy and provided the one bright moment on another bleak afternoon when he ran in a try from 65 metres, a feat which led to sympathetic journalists voting him man of the match, but the 54–9 defeat meant that New Zealand had amassed 155 points against Wales in three matches in a year, winning the try count 26–2.

Those were the days when satellite television was a thing of the future. The WRU, like the Welsh public, was largely reliant on the print and radio broadcast media to relay the sorry tale, unlike

34

today when all Test matches are covered live: reality was distorted by perception. There was no appreciation of how ruthlessly efficient and clinical New Zealand, and their leading provinces, were and the reiterated belief in the Principality that Welsh club rugby was the strongest in the world could not have been more misguided. Wales may have had a dismal touring record, starting in 1964 when they went to South Africa and suffered their biggest defeat for 40 years, 24–3, but the reaction was one of such stunned disbelief that the coaches, Gray and his assistant Derek Quinnell, were held to be responsible. James's warning that the club system had not taken onboard the implications of the switch from grammar to comprehensive schools, and the consequent loss of one-to-one tuition for emerging youngsters, the way Bill Samuel had acted as Gareth Edwards's mentor in the 1960s, had been ignored. His concern that the production line from club to country was in urgent need of repair, because players were technically deficient and lacking the guile which had been the hallmark of Welsh players throughout the game's history, was not shared by the WRU which was content, and relieved, to point the finger at Gray. Whereas Wales had only two coaches in the 1970s, Clive Rowlands and Dawes, they had four in the 1980s and five in the 1990s. The reaction after the defeat to Scotland in 1982 had been to sack Dawes's successor, John Lloyd. Dawes was the last Wales coach to serve his full term until Hansen served out his contract between 2002 and 2004. (Gray was appointed in 1985 after John Bevan had stood down because of illness.)

Before Wales left New Zealand, Jonathan Davies made an impassioned plea to be allowed to speak to the WRU's annual meeting on his return home. He argued that member clubs, and the Union's general committee, needed to be told exactly why the tour had been so calamitous. 'Things must never be the same again in Welsh rugby,' said Davies. 'The game here is totally different: the way players are looked after, able to concentrate on their own training programmes, points the way for us. If we are expected to compete on the field, we have to be given the same facilities off it. I am not sure if people in Wales understand that, which is why I want to give our side of the story. We have as much talent in Wales as they have in New Zealand, but we are light years behind in certain areas, such as most of our forward play. If we act quickly, we can remedy a lot of what has happened in the last month. The tour has wide implications for Welsh rugby. It was not a case of players not trying, nor a lack of ability. We were not competing on the same terms and that must not be allowed to happen again.'

It did, over and over again. The WRU dismissed Davies's plea with disdain and its general committee – which contained Gray among its number – accepted a recommendation from its coaching committee to sack the coaches. 'I could not have been treated with more contempt if I had suggested digging up the National Stadium and planting potatoes,' wrote Davies in his autobiography. 'All I wanted, along with the other players, was to save future Welsh teams from going through our ordeal. The Union merely followed an old Welsh rugby tradition of avoiding criticism by looking for the nearest scapegoat and sacking someone. Getting rid of Tony Gray and Derek Quinnell was a disgraceful act: the best coaches there have ever been would not have stopped the All Blacks from destroying us. The men who had helped us win the Triple Crown a few months earlier were sacrificed. We had been on a suicide mission, deteriorating from European champions to a sad mess without any sign that the WRU had learned any lessons.'

John Ryan, a successful coach at club level with Newport in the 1970s and Cardiff in the early 1980s, succeeded Gray, the first non-international to assume the position, but as the fall-out from the New Zealand tour continued to settle, the Welsh game divided on tribal lines. Neath were the most successful club in the country, but Ryan only chose two of their players for his opening match in charge, against Western Samoa at the National Stadium in November 1988. Wales won 28–6, but for those who hoped that New Zealand marked a nadir in the fortunes of the national side, the next month marked a new low when Romania visited Cardiff. No Neath players were included in the starting line-up, and when Wales lost 15–9 to a side which rarely passed the ball beyond the outside-half, the first time a developing nation had defeated a foundation union in a full international away from home, the result was received by spectators at Neath's next home match two days later with an almost celebratory rapture.

It marked the end for Jonathan Davies who, after several approaches from rugby league clubs, succumbed to an offer from Widnes less than a month after the Romania debacle. 'What made up my mind for me was the realisation that if I stayed in Wales, I would be putting my rugby future in the hands of men I could no longer trust or respect,' he wrote. 'We had advanced no further since New Zealand, in fact we had gone backwards.' Others were to follow: David Young, Paul Moriarty, John Devereux, Rowland Phillips had all turned professional within a year, and by the time Wales played New Zealand in Cardiff in November 1989, Ryan had turned to Neath, who had pushed the All Blacks all the way at the Gnoll a few weeks before, including Thorburn and four of their forwards in his starting line-up. New Zealand were rationed to four tries, but they still enjoyed their biggest victory in the Welsh capital, 34–9. After Wales lost their opening two matches in the 1990 Five Nations Ryan, undermined by a faction within the WRU, resigned and was replaced with unseemly haste by the Neath coach Ron Waldron.

The trigger for Ryan was the 34–6 defeat by England at

Twickenham. It was an embarrassingly inept performance and Ryan, who believed in discipline, felt he had lost the players. He had been in charge for only nine matches and enjoyed a mere two victories. Wales had lost six of their seven championship matches since winning the Triple Crown and though Waldron's first match in charge saw them lose narrowly to the eventual champions Scotland in Cardiff, they ended the season with their first ever Five Nations whitewash and failed to win a match in the 1991 campaign when England prevailed at the Arms Park for the first time since 1963. As Waldron turned more and more to Neath, so animosity towards him built up in east Wales. The squad succumbed to an acrimonious internecine split, culminating in a ruinous tour to Australia that summer.

Wales were crushed 71–8 by New South Wales at the Concord Oval in Sydney before capitulating 63–6 to the Wallabies, a scoreline which would read 75–6 today with a try now worth five points. Neath's style of play, based on superior fitness and an all-action style, may have been enough to sweep all before them in Welsh club rugby, but Waldron's team were regularly out-muscled at forward on the international stage and the backs were little more than tackle bags. As the pressure mounted on the coach, the Neath players in the squad tried to protect him, culminating in a scuffle during the after-match ceremony in Brisbane. 'Whipped, Woeful Wales Wallop Each Other', blazed one local newspaper headline. If, as in 1988, Wales found themselves in the wrong place at the wrong time – Australia went on to win the World Cup five months later – they reflected their governing body, the WRU, lacking direction and looking for someone to blame.

Despite home advantage in the group stage, Wales failed to qualify for the quarter-finals of the World Cup after losing to Western Samoa and Australia. Alan Davies, the former Nottingham and England A coach who had been born in Wales, was in temporary charge for the tournament. After his side had been eliminated at the hands of the Wallabies, 38–3, he said he was not interested in taking on the job full-time because of the various schisms in the Welsh game and he made an impassioned plea for unity. He had been appointed after the WRU had been ready to offer the position to Gray, a move which was thwarted by Ryan, by then a member of the Union's general committee, who argued that the political divide could only be bridged by someone who had had no involvement in the club game and who could, as a consequence, offer a fresh perspective. Davies had left Wales as a boy and, having been overlooked by the Rugby Football Union for the vacant England job a couple of years earlier, was deemed appropriately neutral.

He did remain beyond the 1991 tournament, and was appointed to see Wales through to the end of the 1995 World Cup. And he did make an impact because, three years after the Brisbane brawl, Wales won the Five Nations Championship, failing to secure the Grand Slam after losing to England at Twickenham in their final match. Ultimately, he fell victim to a club system which had remained mediocre despite the introduction of national leagues in 1990, one of the changes instituted as a consequence of the New Zealand tour. The WRU kept tinkering with the league system – constantly increasing or decreasing the number of clubs in the top flight and introducing bonus points in an attempt to encourage more open play – but it steadfastly refused to contemplate reform of itself, quietly shelving the report of a working party set up at the end of the 1980s which recommended, among other proposals, a dismantling of the labyrinthine committee structure, which it deemed did not allow for quick decision-making, and a move towards executive-style administration.

Not even when the general committee was overthrown in a revolution in April 1993, following revelations that it had suppressed the withering conclusions of a report commissioned in 1989 to look into the disproportionate Welsh involvement in a tour arranged to mark the centenary of the South African Rugby Board, did the WRU become streamlined: most of the members who'd had to resign after a vote of no confidence was taken at an extraordinary general meeting of clubs were voted back in a few months later. It was only when the Union's debts, built up after the construction of the Millennium Stadium, threatened to send it into bankruptcy at the end of 2002 that the number of general committee members was reduced. Even then it was not achieved without a bitter fight, which left an unnamed international player quoted as saying that if as much dedication, resolve and resourcefulness had been put into the running of the game, Welsh rugby would not have been reduced to a laughing stock.

There were executive casualties in 1993, while the author of the 1989 report, Vernon Pugh, was elected onto the general committee and was elected its inaugural chairman. Though Alan Davies had restored some pride in the national side, culminating in the 1994 title, he was seen by some on the WRU as embodying English virtues: Wales were no longer a soft touch defensively and they were infinitely more organised, but having reached a level where they were difficult to beat, they struggled to take the next step and take the game to major opponents. The Five Nations Championship was won on the back of a surprise defeat to Canada at the National Stadium, 26–24, a match in which Wales failed to score a try. The evening marked the debut of the number 8 Scott Quinnell, son of the 1970s icon Derek, who was to make his mark in the ensuing championship before he, like many others before him, fell prey to the blandishments of rugby league and joined Wigan.

As happened in 1988, Wales were unable to build on their success and suffered a whitewash in 1995, scoring only one try in their four matches. Pugh and Davies had never enjoyed a cordial relationship, and long before the end of the 1995 championship, Pugh had started to look around for a coach to take over after the World Cup that summer. But, as they had four years before, Wales ended up going to rugby's showpiece event with a caretaker coach in charge. Following the defeat to Ireland at the National Stadium in the final round of matches, J.P.R. Williams, the former Wales full-back, resigned from Davies's selection committee, claiming that the team originally chosen for the game had been changed by the coach without consultation. The WRU called Davies to account and, though it wanted his assistant, Gareth Jenkins, and the team manager Robert Norster to take the squad to South Africa for the World Cup, they refused to break ranks and the three resigned after an overwhelming majority of the general committee failed to give Davies a vote of approval. An Australian, Alex Evans, who was the coach of Cardiff, headed a club triumvirate to take charge of the World Cup campaign: Ruddock, then at Swansea, and Pontypridd's Dennis John made up the trio, but the east-west divide quickly resurfaced and Wales again failed to qualify for the last eight.

It is worth concentrating on modern Welsh rugby history because success, like failure, generates hysteria rather than perspective. Three days after Wales had won the 2005 Grand Slam, the *South Wales Echo* carried a letter from a reader who had been caught up in the magic of the moment. 'Everyone will know the scores of the five victories off by heart, and rightly so, but let us appreciate the way the wins were achieved,' he wrote. 'They did it the Welsh way, playing expansive, exciting and entertaining rugby. Bleddyn Williams, Cliff Morgan et al would have been proud of the flair and bravery on display. That's all we were asking for during the years of Graham Henry and Steve Hansen.' The brio Wales showed during Henry's first year in charge and the flair they showed under Hansen against New Zealand and England, fêted as heroes when they returned home after losing narrowly in the quarter-finals, was drowned in the tidal wave of emotion. 'We have played some very good rugby for the last three years,' said Owen. 'We scored some cracking tries during Steve's time as coach, but they failed to stick in people's memories because we were losing games. Steve Hansen left a tremendous legacy and he was the driving force behind the transformation from losers to winners.'

While the Wales squad and Ruddock paid tribute to Hansen, the Welsh public tended to regard his departure, rather than his 26 months in charge, as the reason for the turnaround. Websites, newspaper columns and radio programmes made constant references to the Welsh style of play, yet for every season like 2005, there have been five when Wales have been distinctly uneasy on the eye. Before this year, Wales's eight Grand Slams had come in clusters: they won three in four seasons from 1908; a 29-year gap followed before two came along almost at once in 1950 and 1952; and there was then a 19-year hiatus before the prize was claimed three times in seven years. In between those periods, such as the first half of the 1960s, Wales were functional and dull. They mustered a mere nine points and no tries in the 1962 Five Nations, drawing 0–0 against England at Twickenham, and 21 points and two tries in 1963, a year when they emerged from a mind-numbing encounter at Murrayfield with a 6–0 victory in a match which, thanks to the Wales scrum-half Clive Rowlands, had produced 111 lineouts.

When the WRU tried in 1967 to recoup some of the costs of turning Cardiff Arms Park into the National Stadium by issuing debentures on a 50-year lease for £50, they were not overwhelmed by demand. Wales had won the Triple Crown in 1965, but in the 1967 and 1968 championships won a solitary match each time. Redemption lay in a crop of talented young players who materialised at around the same time, including Barry John, Gareth Edwards, Gerald Davies, J.P.R. Williams, Maurice Richards, Mervyn Davies and John Taylor. Davies and John made their debuts in 1966, Edwards the following year, along with Morris and Taylor.

Just as it took Hansen two years, and the pain of defeat, to harden his young squad mentally and physically, so it was not until 1969 that Wales recaptured the style of the 1950s, winning the Triple Crown with a 30–9 victory over England at the Arms Park, a match which revealed the true genius of John and the finishing power of Richards, who scored four tries. John's introduction to the international game had been anything but smooth: he was dropped after his first two internationals and only regained his place when David Watkins turned professional. Even the best need time. 'I have identified players I believe are good enough to make an impact in the World Cup,' said Hansen, after announcing his squad for the 2002 summer tour to South Africa, which saw him jettison experience for promise. 'We will find out in the coming year what they are made of and I will be putting performances before results.'

CHAPTER 2

Breaking Down Barriers

Down the ancient corridors, through the gates of time, run the ghosts of days that we have left behind.

Dan Fogelberg

AS THE 2005 SIX NATIONS DAWNED, BOOKMAKERS dismissed Wales's chances of winning the Grand Slam by quoting them at 40–1. A group of former internationals from the four home unions had pooled their knowledge to choose their line-up for the Lions' first Test against New Zealand the following June. Published in the *Sunday Times*, it did not contain a single Wales player. Ruddock, never one to waste a motivational tool, pinned the article on a wall in the players' room at their Vale of Glamorgan base. 'I do not know if it made any difference,' he said later. 'Everyone has an opinion, which is as it should be, and sometimes you can use it to make a point. We were able to ambush sides because we had been written off. When I first took charge of Swansea at the beginning of 1990s, the local newspaper called us "superflops". The article pointed out that it was a long time since we had beaten Llanelli: I stuck it on the wall and told the players I would rip it down when they had defeated them.' It was not up there long.

England were regarded as favourites to prevail on the opening weekend at the Millennium Stadium, even though they had chronic injury problems: Jonny Wilkinson, the totemic outside-half whose extra-time drop goal had taken them to victory in the 2003 World Cup final against Australia in Sydney, was on the treatment table, along with four other players who had been part of that success – Mike Tindall, Will Greenwood, Trevor Woodman and Richard Hill – while Martin Johnson and Lawrence Dallaglio had retired from international rugby. England and France had dominated the championship in the professional era, operating from a stronger commercial base than their Celtic rivals and blessed with strong, competitive domestic leagues which exploited their vastly superior number of players. There were calls for the fixture between England and France to be held permanently on the last weekend of the Six Nations on the grounds that it invariably decided the destiny of the title. The former England second row Paul Ackford, writing in the *Sunday Telegraph*, suggested that England and France should pull out of the championship and ally themselves with the major southern hemisphere nations.

When England defeated Wales in the 2003 World Cup quarter-final, they went ahead in the series of matches between the nations, which stretched back to 1881, for the first time since 1968. They arrived at the Millennium Stadium on 5 February 2005 looking for a record eighth consecutive victory over Wales and had not lost in Cardiff since 1993. Wales had not defeated a major opponent since winning in Paris in the 2001 championship and Ruddock went into his first Six Nations campaign needing to jump a number of hurdles: the dismal run against England in Cardiff; a seven-match losing sequence away from home in the tournament; the failure to beat Ireland in Cardiff since 1983. England and Ireland, for their part, like France, had never lost in the Six Nations at the Millennium Stadium. Weighed down by the past, it was no surprise that Wales were again expected to make up the numbers, even in a year when the lustre of England's World Cup triumph had tarnished with six defeats in their previous nine Tests and when France, under their maverick coach Bernard Laporte, appeared to be more concerned with the 2007 World Cup which they were hosting than retaining their championship crown.

For Ruddock, history became his story. When the WRU had opened its centenary celebrations with a whimper as the All Blacks marched to victory at the National Stadium in 1980, it was Wales's 50th defeat at home in a full international; when Ruddock took charge of Wales for the first time in a match at the Millennium Stadium, against South Africa in November 2004, the 38–36 loss was their 100th at home: the first 50 had taken 98 years, the second a mere 25. The increased number of fixtures offered only a partial explanation. Wales had, for a generation, lost the art of winning consistently, offering knee-jerk reactions to failure; it took Hansen, a New Zealander, to change the mind-set, and even then the nerve of the WRU nearly failed it. When Wales lost to England in a pre-World Cup friendly in August 2003, a match arranged as a commercial exercise to help compensate for the loss of revenue because, with the World Cup taking place in Australia that October and November, there would be no autumn internationals, it was their tenth reverse in a row under Hansen, who at that stage had nine months to run on his contract. He was called in by the powers-that-be and warned that if the forthcoming friendly against Scotland ended in defeat, he faced the sack. The

World Cup may only have been weeks away, but the Union had a history of dumping coaches just before the big event and, for the first time since he had taken over from Graham Henry in February 2002, the result counted for infinitely more than the performance that Hansen had been forever trumpeting.

The WRU was reacting to public and commercial pressure. Hansen deliberately cultivated a dour public image: one of his first acts after succeeding Henry was to call a meeting with the Welsh media at a hotel in the centre of Cardiff to lay down ground rules. Whereas Henry invited contact, day or night, and was always available for a quote, Hansen said he did not want any unsolicited calls on his mobile telephone. Any interviews had to be arranged in advance through the WRU's media officer at the time, Lyn Davies. Anyone who misquoted him would be held to account. He made it clear that he would do what was required of him, but no more. He had seen the way the press corps had hounded Henry with a mounting hostility, despite the courtesies he had extended to them, and had no intention of wasting time trying to ingratiate himself with opinion formers in the media.

Henry had brought Hansen over from New Zealand, where he had been part of a successful coaching team at Canterbury Crusaders, in response to Wales's failure to make a sustained impact on the world stage. Henry's dream from the day he arrived in Cardiff was to get Wales into the top five world rankings, and his initial approach was entirely hands-on. He had an assistant coach, Lynn Howells; a conditioning expert in the Geordie Steve Black; and a selector in Allan Lewis, then the Newport director of rugby, but there was no questioning who was in charge. Soon after Henry's appointment, the WRU ran a poster campaign which proclaimed him as The Great Redeemer, a tag which stuck when Wales went on their winning run in 1999, never mind that the central lesson of the previous ten years had been that no one man could cure Welsh rugby of its many ills. By offering Henry an annual salary of £250,000 and a five-year contract, the WRU was effectively looking for a magician with an endless supply of wands. 'We are in the last-chance saloon,' said Glanmor Griffiths, who had taken over from Pugh as the WRU chairman, 'and we have secured the services of the best coach in the world.' It was all Henry could do, coming from a country where sentiment and emotion play no part in rugby, to stop himself surfing on the wave of euphoria which broke after his first game in charge, against South Africa at Wembley in November 1998, had ended in an honourable defeat after Wales had taken a 14-point lead a mere five months after the 96–13 humiliation in Pretoria.

Henry, who had made his coaching name with Auckland and then with the Super 12 franchise the Auckland Blues, had been approached by England in 1997. He turned them down after the Rugby Football Union's interest was made public, but he proved more amenable when Wales came calling. Henry was 52 in 1998, and although he was in charge of the New Zealand A side, his long-held ambition of coaching the All Blacks was looking increasingly forlorn with younger rivals coming through the system, while by that point the Blues looked to have climbed their mountain and to be coming down the other side. His detractors were to later claim that Henry had only come to Wales for the money; while few would have turned down a salary which at the time was greater than that enjoyed by any other Test coach, his prime motivation was to take charge of an international side. 'I did not feel I was close to the New Zealand job,' he was to say later. 'The All Blacks remain the pinnacle of my ambition, and when I accepted the Wales job the New Zealand Rugby Union drew up a rule which prevented anyone who opted to coach abroad from ever being involved with the All Blacks. It was a hasty over-reaction to my decision: I had been left with the choice of staying at home in hope or accepting an offer to test myself at international level. Wales, like New Zealand, is a country where rugby is the national sport. My time there may not have ended as I intended, but I will always be grateful for the opportunity they gave me.' Less than two years after returning to New Zealand in 2002, Henry succeeded John Mitchell as the New Zealand coach. The so-called Henry rule had been shelved after a fourth successive abortive World Cup campaign and he became the first man to head the coaching set-ups of two foundation unions.

Wales turned to Henry after Kevin Bowring, who had taken over as the Wales coach in the autumn of 1995 and then left by mutual consent following a shattering Five Nations campaign in 1998. Wales defeated Scotland and Ireland, but they conceded a record 60 points against England at Twickenham and were humiliated 51–0 by France at Wembley. Bowring, a former London Welsh flanker who had made his coaching reputation with Wales at Under-21 level, was an intellectual coach in the mould of Tony Gray. Appreciating that the system was hindering rather than helping him, the manner of the defeat against France encouraged him to draw up a list of ten policies he wanted the WRU to implement. Those on the Union who wanted to be rid of him interpreted the recommendations as an ultimatum and, for the fifth time in ten years, the WRU parted company with a coach. Bowring knew the task required was too big for one man but the WRU, declaring that money was no object, declared its intention to trawl the world for his successor rather than to look to spread the load.

The search got no further than the other side of the Irish Sea. Ruddock, who had left Wales the previous year to become Leinster's director of coaching, was asked if he would be interested in taking over from Bowring. He accepted with alacrity, subject to the details of his contract, and in May 1998, the WRU's technical committee had a monthly meeting which had the position of Wales coach at the top of its agenda; if it put forward Ruddock's name, the recommendation would have to be ratified by the Union's general committee, which was gathering later that day. Ruddock's elevation appeared to be a foregone conclusion, so much so that Pugh, a barrister who, although no longer the WRU chairman because his election as the chairman of the International Rugby Board precluded him from occupying a position of authority on his union, remained the central figure on the governing body, had chosen not to attend either meeting, having travelled to his chambers in London.

On the morning of the two meetings, Pugh suddenly decided to return to Wales. 'I felt that we were rushing things unnecessarily,' he said later. 'We had promised to take our time and look throughout the world for a coach and we had not done that. What concerned me most was that the game was becoming increasingly political [Cardiff and Swansea were to pull out of the Welsh League and the Heineken Cup that year to play unofficial friendlies against the leading English clubs in protest at the way the game was being administered in Wales]. To have dropped a Welsh coach, albeit one who had been in Ireland for a year, into that mire would, I felt, have minimised his chances of succeeding. There was no question in my mind that Mike Ruddock had the credentials to become the Wales coach, but it seemed more prudent at a time of such upheaval to turn to an outsider who would be better able to tiptoe his way through the minefield. The more I thought about it, the more I felt that Mike should be the successor to our next coach. That is why I caught the train back to Cardiff and recommended that we widen our search to the southern hemisphere. In retrospect, I think it was the right course of action. Graham Henry had clout in the WRU's corridors of power which would have been denied to

Mike at that time.'

Pugh was given Henry's name by Lee Smith, a New Zealander who worked for the International Rugby Board. As Wales prepared for their fateful Test against the Springboks, Griffiths, the WRU secretary Dennis Gethin and the Union's technical director Terry Cobner flew to Sydney for a clandestine meeting with Henry, the first two from London and the last from Johannesburg. 'When we were in transit in Singapore and when I saw the score from Pretoria, I turned to Glanmor and said we may as well turn back and fly home,' said Gethin. 'I could not see any way Henry would leave behind what he had in New Zealand to take on what appeared to be a hopeless cause.'

In fact, if anything, the size of the task he faced appealed to Henry. His coaching career had largely been one of uninterrupted success: Auckland won 80 of their 102 matches under him between 1992 and 1997, while he led the Blues to the Super 12 championship title in 1996 and 1997 and they finished runners-up in 1998.

Henry blew into Wales like a gale-force wind. Whereas Bowring and Alan Davies had been kept at arm's length by the Union's general committee, summoned to meetings rather than being allowed to attend them as of right, Henry came and went as he pleased. Asked not to watch any of Cardiff's or Swansea's rebel matches against English opposition, he turned up at the Arms Park for the game against Saracens, occupying a prominent seat and generating considerable publicity. Henry enjoyed considerably more power than any of his predecessors and exploited it to the full. The lack of checks and balances on him was later to rebound on the WRU, which became entangled in the Grannygate affair of 2000 when it was revealed that the New Zealanders Shane Howarth and Brett Sinkinson, capped by Henry, were ineligible to play for Wales. As his Redeemer image faded and as Wales started to lose matches again by embarrassing margins, those on the general committee who had resented Henry's perceived accretion of power and lack of accountability started to try to rein him in. Henry continued to trample on political toes, urging the abandonment of the club system which had underpinned the Welsh game for some 120 years and its replacement by regional rugby. There were nine clubs in the top division of the Welsh League; on average, they enjoyed only one-third of the funding of their English counterparts. As the standard of the club game declined, so Henry became increasingly aware that he needed help.

He looked across the Severn Bridge with envy at the England head coach Clive Woodward. He had assembled an army of coaches who were given free rein to concentrate on their specialist areas. Although Wales had defeated England at Wembley at the end of Henry's first championship, a late try by Scott Gibbs and a conversion by Neil Jenkins edging them home by a point, they had been routed in each of the subsequent two years. When he took charge of the Lions in Australia in 2001, Henry was backed up by three of the England coaching team: Andy Robinson, Woodward's assistant, Phil Larder, whose speciality was defence, and Dave Alred, a kicking guru. When he returned to Wales, he decreed that Wales should go down the same route. Money was a problem with the WRU struggling to pay the interest on its debt, never mind making any inroads into the £70 million it owed, but Henry succeeded in securing the appointment of Hansen and that of Scott Johnson, who had been part of the Australia A management team which had masterminded a victory over the Lions.

Henry's attitude to his players bordered on the authoritarian. He acted like the schoolmaster he had been, keeping his distance. Players very often learned why they had been left out of, or had been included in, a side through Henry's remarks during media conferences. While there was respect for him, there was little in the way of affection and when he returned from Australia, the player-coach relationship changed. Ten Welsh players had been chosen for the tour, more than their performances in that year's Six Nations had justified, and the majority of them did not figure in his Test plans. They, even more than their English, Scottish and Irish counterparts, resented being shunted into the midweek sidings without a word of explanation. Henry was not used to having to massage egos, and was not prepared to give it a go. The rift which had opened up with key members of his squad was revealed in defeats that autumn against Ireland and Argentina at the Millennium Stadium, and though Wales then ran Australia close, a 50-point hammering by Ireland in Dublin the following February pushed him over the edge. Even though he was putting together a structure which would have seen him head a coaching pyramid and so devolve his responsibilities, he had nothing left to give mentally.

Just as Hansen deserved his share of the credit for the 2005 Grand Slam, so Henry should be acknowledged for the systems he put in place. When he arrived in Wales, he was surprised to find so many of the players lacking on the technical front. 'It was a shock at my first few training sessions to find that basic skills, such as taking and receiving a pass, were not there,' he said. 'It made you wonder just what was going on in the schools and clubs. What there was in Wales was a huge enthusiasm for the game: success on the rugby field stirred the national consciousness, but too many obstacles were put in the way of progress. Being part of it was both uplifting and frustrating: you could see the potential, but realising that potential was another matter.'

Henry was used to players who thought for themselves. He

became so exasperated with his forwards' play at the breakdown, where organisation and understanding often appeared to be lacking, that he devised a pod system. In essence, it divided the pack into two after a set-piece: one group would join in the breakdown when a player was tackled while the other unit would spread out in the back line. Henry's plan covered multiple phases, but it proved too complicated for the players and the coach ended up being ridiculed in the media. 'There was nothing wrong with the system,' said Martyn Williams. 'The problem was that in those days we lacked the fitness and the skills to do it justice. We still use pods, though for only two or three phases now because we are better equipped to play with our heads up. The impact of Scott Johnson has been to improve the skills of every player in the squad: the way the forwards handled and passed during the championship, able to do both at pace, summed up how we have come on over the last four years. Many people put our improvement down to the fact that a Welshman is in charge again: Mike is a superb coach who has improved our set-piece play considerably, but I would not put our displays down to Welshness. A lot of moves we put together were born on the training field: the key was that we had the confidence to play at a high, sustained tempo because of our victory over England in the first game. We were not at our best then, but the win was everything. We had come close to South Africa and New Zealand in the November and had had a number of near misses under Steve. We needed one big scalp to light the fuse and we finally got it.'

On the surface, Hansen did not appear to be an ideal candidate to replace Henry. The accent was the same and he appeared to live up to the stereotype of a humourless South Islander. Henry had a permanent half-smile on his face and liked to josh with journalists in media conferences. For the first 18 months of Henry's reign, Black offered a shoulder to cry on for the players. He had arrived from Newcastle Falcons, where he had been Jonny Wilkinson's mentor, and bubbled with infectious enthusiasm. He maintained that fitness was as much mental as it was physical and did not believe in testing players because poor results would undermine confidence. He preferred to get inside heads, and while Henry was never regarded as an agony uncle, players poured out all their troubles to Black. When the fitness coach, concerned that media criticism of his methods had started to affect his family, decided to return to the north-east in March 2000, Henry was never going to be able to find another Black.

Hansen's approach was completely different. Distant with the media, though he gradually gathered a few confidants, he developed a close bond with his players. A former policeman, he had the reputation of being a good friend and a bad enemy. He was concerned that cliques had developed by the end of the Henry era and that a number of players were more concerned with themselves than the team. Though he only made two voluntary changes for his first match in charge, at home to France, a game which came to sum up his period in charge, ending in a narrow defeat after Scott Quinnell had fallen within inches of the line in the dying minutes to be denied what would have been the winning score, he injected young blood into the tour to South Africa that summer when, against all expectations, Wales twice pushed the Springboks close. Two fixtures in the 2005 side were given their first starts: the scrum-half Dwayne Peel and the number 8 Michael Owen, who played at blind-side flanker. Both players had been identified by Henry as future internationals, though he thought Owen would make a better second row.

'I have nothing but praise for Steve Hansen,' said Owen. 'He seemed to be deliberately dour to the media, but he was totally different when he was with the players. He drew us close together and was always approachable: if you had a problem you would never hesitate to go to him. He worked the squad really hard in South Africa because he wanted us to be successful. He said he wanted to leave a legacy, and he succeeded in that, as we showed in the Six Nations. As soon as we had won the Grand Slam, he was on the phone telling us to make sure that we had our ice baths! He said we had the ability to win the championship again and that is what we intend to do. Mike Ruddock was able to build on what Steve had left him.'

The catalyst for Hansen was the 2003 World Cup group match against New Zealand. Wales had already qualified for the quarter-finals, but having put away Canada with ease, they laboured against Tonga and Italy. Hansen wanted them to express themselves but, like Gray in 1988, struggled to find the means. If Gray's solution was a player appearing out of position at full-back, so it was with Hansen, who had mixed up his team for the All Blacks. A thrashing was predicted by the media, who were not prepared for the most entertaining match of the tournament. New Zealand took an early lead when the wing Joe Rokocoko finished off a polished move, but the game turned when the Wales full-back Garan Evans left the field injured shortly after. Gareth Thomas, a vastly experienced player, whose caps had come in the centre or on the wing, came off the bench. 'If I had had time to think about it, I would have been a nervous wreck,' said Thomas, a player who had had a chequered career under Henry with the coach seeming to misinterpret the player's exuberance and outgoing nature for immaturity and unreliability. 'I told the boys that with me at full-back there was no point in keeping it tight – we had to go for it. We scored a couple of tries and our confidence surged. We still lost, and that was hard to take after being in the lead for so long, but we had proved to ourselves and to the world that we could take the game to a top team.'

Wales had again leaked a half-century of points, but the 37 they scored marked their highest ever total against the All Blacks. Suddenly the WRU, which a couple of months beforehand had handed Hansen an ultimatum – win, or else – was talking about extending his contract. Hansen had long declared his intention to return to New Zealand the following May for family reasons, and was not to be swayed. 'There was some grief when we lost the friendly to England and there was pressure on us in the Scotland game,' said Hansen. 'I always maintained that those August matches would not take precedence over our preparations for the World Cup. We did not want them, but the WRU clearly needed the money and we had no option but to play them. When I took over, I took a long-term view: it was going to take at least two years to get Wales near to where I wanted them, starting with the tour to South Africa. There were times when we came under pressure to bring in experienced players to help end the run of defeats, but that would not have achieved anything. I was happy to take the flak because I knew that the squad we were developing was going to become special. People will always have opinions in rugby, and as the Wales coach you know you are going to be the focus of attention. The style of play we showed against New Zealand in the World Cup did not happen by accident: when I brought in the fitness coach Andrew Hore from New Zealand in 2002, he put together a two-year programme. With Scott Johnson working on skills, everyone knew the game we wanted. It was just not going to come together overnight.'

Wales had suffered their first Six Nations whitewash in 2003, starting their campaign with a first ever defeat to Italy in Rome. The previous summer, Hansen had made the flanker Colin Charvis his captain. It was a controversial choice: Charvis had been dropped from the squad for Henry's last game for choosing to go on a family holiday rather than attend a training session. Charvis was vilified in the media, even though there were mitigating circumstances in his case: when he had booked the holiday, which he had arranged so that he could take his sister back to their family roots in Jamaica, he was told that the weekend was free of national commitments. When he was taken off in the second half in Rome, a television camera appeared to catch him in the dug-out smiling, prompting another wave of media indignation. The result meant that Wales's only victims in 16 Tests had been Tonga, Italy (in 2002), Romania, Fiji and Canada. Hansen did turn to one old stager for the next match against England at the Millennium Stadium, recalling the 33-year-old hooker Jonathan Humphreys to lead the side with Charvis dropped to the bench. The result was a vastly improved display against the World Cup winners in waiting, even if the next victory would have to wait until the following August when a largely second-string Wales side, coached by Ruddock because Hansen was preparing for the friendly against Scotland three days later, thrashed Romania in Wrexham, with a wing who had been out of the picture for nearly two years, Shane Williams, marking his recall with two tries which earned him a place in the World Cup squad.

The class of 2005 contained only two players who had not featured under Hansen – the flanker Ryan Jones and the prop John Yapp. Every back who started the final match against Ireland had been capped by Henry. For the first time since the 1970s, the transition from one coach to another had been seamless, a point missed by those who hailed the Grand Slam as proof that Wales were well rid of the two New Zealanders. Ruddock had put the roof on the house built by Hansen on the foundation laid by Henry.

CHAPTER 3

White Out

Winning is not everything. It is the only
thing.

Vince Lombardi

THE WEATHER IN CARDIFF ON 5 FEBRUARY 2005 WAS AS
bleak as it had been on 6 February 1993, the last time Wales had
defeated England at the National Stadium. On this occasion, the
Millennium Stadium at least had a roof to keep the elements at
bay, although the newly laid surface was to cut up as badly as
Wembley used to during the International Horse of the Year Show.
'Just Do It,' blared the headline in that morning's *Western Mail*, a
mildly despairing reference to Wales's sequence of near misses
since Hansen's first match in charge. The trend had continued
under Ruddock the previous November: South Africa, the Tri-
Nations champions, had won by two points after Wales, who
showed the dividends of the work put in under their fitness coach
Andrew Hore, had been trailing 38–22 with eight minutes of

normal time remaining. Late tries by Henson and Peel, two players who were to have a profound influence on the destiny of the Six Nations Championship, left the Springboks relieved to hear the final whistle, having mistakenly believed that the stadium clock stopped on every occasion the referee called time off. Ruddock's team had included six Joneses: Stephen, Duncan, Steve, Adam, Dafydd and Ryan, with the coach hoping that South Africa would not be able to keep up with them. 'It is no secret that Wales play best when we have tempo and width in our game,' Ruddock had said before the match. Crucial to his gameplan was the need for an inside-centre in the mould of a New Zealand second five-eighth, a player who complemented his outside-half with his range of passing and kicking skills, an extra attacking, rather than a defensive, option.

'I sat down with Scott Johnson at the start of the season and talked about the style of play Wales had adopted during the 2003 World Cup,' said Ruddock, on a BBC Radio Wales phone-in after the end of the championship. 'A key factor then was the presence of a second-five in Iestyn Harris and we felt that the way forward for the team was to reproduce that style of rugby; as Iestyn had returned to rugby league, we needed to find a player in a similar mould to him. What I did not want was a contact player: we looked around and decided that our best way forward was to put Gavin in there. It was a contentious decision and I received a number of letters saying we were going down the wrong road. There are times when you have to make a big call and we got this one right. We were not going to win any arm-wrestles up front, though we certainly improved in that area; a lot of teams were going for contact, and with defences so well organised in the modern game, our plan was to avoid contact as much as possible and off-load in the tackle.'

After Wales had secured the Grand Slam, Stuart Davies, a

thinking number 8 who had won 17 caps in the 1990s, posed an interesting question: would Wales have won it had the previous coach remained in charge? 'I am of the opinion that that would not have been the case,' argued Davies. 'I know from my time as a player at Swansea under Mike how he can inspire a side and he has taken the team on to a higher level. I have always believed that you need a Welsh coach standing in front of players as they prepare to go out on to the field.' It is worth distilling his question: would Wales have beaten England had Steve Hansen still been the coach? Would he have chosen Henson in the centre?

The key to the Grand Slam was the victory over England. The only time Wales showed appreciable signs of nerves during the tournament was during the second half of that match. They had led 8–3 at the interval after having scored an 11th-minute try, which was a sign of things to come: Wales had squeezed England at a lineout, Martyn Williams then stole the throw and, after play had quickly been taken through a couple of phases, Henson found Michael Owen and it was the number 8's precise long pass which gave Shane Williams the time to squeeze in at the corner.

England, beset by injuries, did not arrive in Cardiff armed with a sense of adventure: they had chosen two outside-centres in their midfield, the Newcastle pair of Jamie Noon and the uncapped 18-year-old Mathew Tait, and they anticipated achieving a dominance in the set-pieces. Their coach, Andy Robinson, had recalled the experienced scrum-half Matt Dawson, a 1997 and 2001 Lion who had been dropped from the England squad in the run-up to the autumn internationals for putting his television commitments – he was a panellist on the BBC's *A Question of Sport* – before a Red Rose training session, to bolster the outside-half Charlie Hodgson; and initially it was Dawson who called all the shots.

Robinson had originally appointed Jonny Wilkinson as his

captain the previous October, but the Newcastle outside-half, who had not long recovered from a career-threatening neck and shoulder injury, was back in the treatment room after taking repeated knocks on his right biceps. Wilkinson had become a national treasure after his winning drop goal in the 2003 World Cup final, and while England missed the imposing presence and inspiration of Martin Johnson, their captain that day, together with the collective experience and wisdom of their back row trio of Lawrence Dallaglio, Richard Hill and Neil Back, it is arguable that at the start of the Six Nations Championship in Cardiff, the individual they most grieved for was Wilkinson.

While Robinson had to make do without the successors to the retired Dallaglio and Back, Leicester's Martin Corry and Lewis Moody, who were both injured, the loss of Wilkinson, who had recovered from his biceps problem only to strain knee ligaments playing for Newcastle against Perpignan in the Heineken Cup three weeks before the start of the Six Nations, affected the balance of the back division. Hodgson was a more naturally gifted player than Wilkinson, a perfectionist who was driven by ambition, but he lacked his rival's mental strength. When England defeated South Africa 32–16 in November, with Hodgson scoring 27 points and landing all his kicks, observers asked whether Wilkinson's future with England, if he still had one, did not in fact lie at inside-centre. The following week, Australia targeted Hodgson, using the burly number 8 David Lyons to charge at him in the opening minutes and England found themselves in disarray defensively, 12–0 down after 30 minutes, by which time Robinson had taken off his inside-centre Henry Paul and replaced him with the experienced Will Greenwood.

Paul, who, like Hodgson, had impressed against the Springboks, had made a couple of errors in defence and attack, but on the surface it seemed a drastic measure to humiliate a player by taking him off so early. He appeared to be a sacrifice for Hodgson: at 31, and with Wilkinson expected to be fit long before the start of the Six Nations, Paul appeared to be expendable in a way that Hodgson, a 24 year old who would be around in the 2007 World Cup and beyond, was not. Greenwood, a member of the World Cup-winning side and the holder of more than 50 caps, was charged with stiffening England's mental resolve. Hodgson had two penalties in the final five minutes of the opening half, the first from 25 metres and the second from 30. Neither was wide-angled, but as he placed the ball each time, the Australian players closest to him started to sledge him, offering their opinion that they did not think that the touch judges were going to be raising their flags. And they didn't.

Hodgson did not take another kick at goal. When England had an early second-half penalty in the Australia 22, Hodgson did not offer his captain, Jason Robinson, the option of three points, dropping to the ground and clutching his knee. It was hard to imagine Wilkinson in the same circumstances not giving Robinson a choice, whatever his physical condition: he had missed three drop goal attempts in the World Cup final, but he was never one to be deterred by failure. As it was, England kicked for touch and scored a try from the resulting lineout. Hodgson did not take the conversion and limped off ten minutes before the end. 'We set out to go at Hodgson from the start,' said the Australia coach Eddie Jones. 'We felt we could unsettle him.' The Wallabies' second row Justin Harrison was less diplomatic after his side's 21–19 victory. 'We were delighted that Wilkinson was not playing,' he said.

As Robinson prepared for the Six Nations, he had a dilemma at half-back and in the centre. Greenwood would not be available for the entire campaign, having had surgery on a shoulder, while the outside-centre Mike Tindall, another World Cup-winner, was out with a foot injury. Robinson had kept Paul, a second-five, in the squad, and he had the option of the 23-year-old Bath centre Olly Barkley, another outside-half by preference. With his outside-centres – Tait, Ollie Smith and Noon – all raw at international level, the only experienced midfielder at his disposal was the 33-year-old Mike Catt, who had been dropped from the squad the previous autumn having been part of the World Cup squad, coming off the bench at half-time to help turn the quarter-final against Wales after Wilkinson had struggled, under intense pressure, to impose himself tactically. Catt would hardly have been a long-term solution, but by opting to go for experience at scrum-half rather than inside-centre, Robinson was taking the prime decision-making responsibility away from the midfield and the way England started in Cardiff, using Dawson to box kick, even from his own 22, did not surprise Wales. It was only when Barkley came on in the final quarter to replace the unfortunate Tait, who had twice been picked up and driven back in the tackle by Henson – on the second occasion casually lifted up as if he were a shop window dummy – that England started to play an effective territorial game. But it was 60 minutes too late.

Hodgson only missed one kick in Cardiff, from 30 metres in first-half stoppage time after he had placed the ball in such a way that it looked bound to fall over. It was to prove decisive, with his side losing by two points, the margin by which Australia had defeated them, while the following week England were to go down against France by one point after Hodgson and Barkley had missed six kicks at goal between them. Hodgson did have a late chance to sink the French, lining up for a drop goal attempt from virtually the same position as that in which Wilkinson found himself at the end of the World Cup final. Hodgson was not rushed into the kick, but he hooked it so badly that it would not have gone through an adjacent set of posts. 'Hodgson lacks self-confidence compared to Wilkinson,' said the France defence coach Dave Ellis. 'We knew that, unlike Wilkinson, Hodgson does not like going into contact. He prefers to stand deeper and, when we rushed up on him in a line, he took a step backwards before unloading the ball and put his runners under pressure.'

The day before the international between Wales and England, Gerald Davies had written in *The Times*: 'Gavin Henson is unlike any other rugby player plying his trade. His style of play is unique. In his ambition, too, he departs from the rest. His *Pop Idol* appearance serves to confirm his essential distinctiveness. With the soft features of the comeback Elvis Presley, his exotic good looks, his gelled, spiky hairstyle – once coloured to match his silver boots – Henson is not your regular rugby player from the Ogwr Valley. He sports a mischievous glamour . . . but his outward appearance should not mislead anyone into believing that he does not have the fibre to survive the tough temper and turbulence of rugby. He is independently and refreshingly his own man – open and honest. He is made of stern stuff and yet has a delicacy of touch that finds no equivalent outside of France at their best.'

Like Hodgson, Henson's international career started in 2001. He was chosen as a 19 year old for the tour to Japan: Wales had taken the opportunity to blood a number of young players with a full side either unavailable through injury or because they were with the Lions in Australia. He came on as a replacement for the full-back Kevin Morgan during the first Test and the following September he started at outside-half in an evening international against Romania at the Millennium Stadium. While Graham Henry had carefully nurtured the wing Shane Williams after he had started his international career with a flourish, trying to shield him from a media he believed was always on the look-out for the next hero, only to dump him when he showed signs of mortality, the New Zealander had other things on his mind by the time

Henson burst on to the scene. Henson struggled from the start against Romania, and it was only when he went off injured and Stephen Jones moved from centre to outside-half that Wales shifted into overdrive. Henson faded back into the relative obscurity of the Welsh league with Swansea, a club which had entered a period of decline, beset with financial problems and reflecting the woes of the Welsh domestic game. His period in the wilderness lasted 21 months and, coincidentally, spanned 21 Tests.

Henry left the Wales job having failed to figure out where Henson's best position was. The player himself preferred outside-half, where he had played most of his rugby, but standing at 6 ft and weighing 15 st., he appeared to Henry to offer greater possibilities at full-back, a position he felt had not been adequately filled since the enforced departure of Shane Howarth following the Grannygate scandal the previous year. Henson found himself in a vacuum when Hansen replaced Henry, unable to prove himself in a club running out of money and jettisoning its most expensive players, and there were concerns that he would go off the rails.

'I did a lot of socialising at the time and went out more than I should have done,' said Henson before the November 2004 international against South Africa, his first start in Wales since Romania three years before. 'A number of the older players at Swansea did the same, but I came to realise that to succeed as a professional I had to make sacrifices. It was difficult at first because my friends were at university and spent nights enjoying themselves, but there is no point in trying to make a career in rugby if you do not want to make it your total focus and there will be plenty of time to go out when I have retired. A turning-point for me was when the regional system replaced the old club structure: it was hard to play behind a beaten pack all the time at

Swansea. Some of us were put on half wages while others, including the head coach John Connolly, who had a fund of great ideas, were sacked. I felt I was good enough to be still playing for Wales, but it was frustratingly difficult to prove that to the selectors. People say that I was capped too early, but I disagree with that. I wondered if I had a future in Wales, and I considered moving to England, but I never stopped believing in myself. That kept me going, but it will always annoy me that I missed out on 20-odd caps.'

Henson made only two appearances in the Hansen era, as a replacement for the wing Tom Shanklin during the 55–3 defeat to New Zealand in Hamilton in the summer of 2003, having helped Wales to an Under-21 Grand Slam, and as full-back against Romania the following August. He was not chosen in the squad for the World Cup that autumn and played no part in the 2004 Six Nations. While Hansen, like Ruddock, believed in the virtues of having a second-five, he used Iestyn Harris in that position. The question of whether he would have chosen Henson to fill the role vacated by Harris is unanswerable. As Ruddock settled on the idea after consulting with his skills coach Scott Johnson, who had been Hansen's right-hand man, it is arguable that the same decision would have been reached by Hansen. By last November, Henson had helped his region, Neath-Swansea Ospreys, to the top of the Celtic League and the only alternative as a second-five was Stephen Jones, which would have meant moving him from outside-half and bringing in Ceri Sweeney.

The main reservation Hansen would have had about Henson was that he loathed the cult of the celebrity. To him, a team was only as strong as its weakest member, not its most talented or fêted. Henson, with his penchant for elaborately spiking his hair and shaving his body, could have passed for a film star. Nearly 50 years before, the Cross Keys' forward Rex Richards won his first

– and only – cap as a prop against France, a position he had never played in before. A long international career beckoned, but he left Wales for North America and fame soon after. 'His first job was as a professional diver, leaping off a 125-ft tower in the Gulf of Mexico,' wrote the club's historian, Horace Jefferies, in his history of Cross Keys. 'He acted as a stuntman in films that contained dramatic water scenes and played the role of King Wongo in the film *The Wild Women of Wongo*, before breaking into television and landing the part of an Indian brave in the television series *Hawkeye*.' Richards, whose nickname was Tarzan because of the cry he gave when diving from a high platform, was a showman who wanted to see the world; Henson is a showman who wants the world to see him.

Of course, he is much more than a showman. 'When I took charge of Swansea, Gavin was a very shy young man,' said Connolly, who became Bath's head coach after leaving Swansea. 'We got him a job at a local hotel to help him improve his communication skills: they would make sure that he chatted to people, and although he did not stay there for long, it did bring something out of him. What I noticed in the Six Nations, and it thrilled me, was that his passion for Wales's jersey shone through. He looked comfortable on the international field and there was another dimension to him. I know that he prefers to play at outside-half, but I feel inside-centre should remain his position. Communication is still something he has to work on because it is a fundamental tool for a fly-half. By not making him the main goal-kicker and keeping Stephen Jones at outside-half, Mike Ruddock has taken some of the pressure and responsibility off Gavin and allowed him to play his natural game.

'The fact that Gavin is fastidious about his appearance should not mask his steely determination. At Swansea, he used to iron his socks, even for training, and there was never a crease in his jersey.

WHITE OUT

Fame came early for him and, at the start, he had trouble coping with everything it brought in its wake. He was better prepared the second time around and he has been handled well by Ruddock and Scott Johnson. I have never seen anyone able to kick a ball as far as Gavin, out of hand or from the ground. When he lined up the late penalty against England, I never had any doubt that it was going over. I had never seen him miss one from long-distance. There are still things he has to work on: his front-on tackling is fierce, as he showed when dealing with Tait, but he is more vulnerable side-on, something France looked to exploit. He is a young man who, at the age of 23, has the rugby world at his feet and in his hands.'

He certainly had a number of England ball-carriers in his hands in his first appearance in the championship before dropping them at his feet, and not just the hapless Tait. Even the burly prop Julian White was given a speed lesson in the laws of gravity as Henson strode the Millennium Stadium as if on a one-man crusade. It was the moment he had been craving all his career: centre-stage with tens of millions of viewers looking on. When the end came, it was as if it had been scripted for him.

England had gradually clawed their way back in the second half. Hodgson had made it 8–6 with his second penalty after 49 minutes, and when Barkley came on the balance of the game seemed to shift. Wales were unsure whether to defend their lead or to look to extend it. Martyn Williams had said three days before the match that one of the reasons that they had been unable to apply the killer punch under Hansen was their inability to get two scores ahead. 'We used to lose sight of how we had got into a good position and would start to play more conservatively. If we take the lead against England, we have to make sure we score next,' he said. England were the only side on the day to follow up one score with another, Hodgson's third penalty giving England a

9–8 lead with seven minutes remaining, a scoreline with a disturbing historical resonance for the Welsh.

Those who remembered the last golden era would have been forgiven for casting their minds back 25 years to Twickenham when hopes of a fourth successive Triple Crown came to grief in controversial circumstances. Wales had to play the last 66 minutes with 14 men after the flanker Paul Ringer had been sent off by the Irish referee David Burnett for a high tackle on the England outside-half John Horton. The act itself was not especially deserving of an early bath, but the match had started rancorously when the England number 8, John Scott, started a fight with his Cardiff club-mate, the Wales scrum-half Terry Holmes, virtually from the kick-off and Burnett had had to call the captains together after just five minutes to instruct them to cool their players down. When that failed to restore order, Burnett warned that the next miscreant would walk and the unfortunate Ringer found himself on his way to the dressing-room and infamy. It was an episode which was to have long-term ramifications for Welsh rugby: the media build-up to the match had been unusually hostile with lavish attention paid to the alleged indiscipline of the Welsh forwards and the perceived barbarity of the Welsh game; it was a time when a number of English clubs had cancelled fixtures against Welsh sides in protest at alleged acts of violence. When Wales returned from their 1988 visit to New Zealand and held an inquest into a humiliating month, the tour manager Rod Morgan cited the Ringer match as one of the reasons for the decline of the national side: the subsequent attempt to clean up the game had failed to differentiate between hard and dirty play, in his view, and had led to a decline in uncompromising forward play which was not as aggressive as it had been.

Wales made light of their one-man disadvantage in 1980 and looked to have secured victory when the wing Elgan Rees scampered over to put his side 8–6 in front five minutes from time. Stoppage time was being played when Holmes strayed offside and England were awarded a penalty. Up stepped their full-back Dusty Hare, who the following year was to blow the chance to take England to their first victory in Cardiff for 18 years when he missed a last-minute penalty.

Hare's kick, 22 metres out but from a wide angle, was less demanding than Henson's match-winner a quarter of a century on, but the pressure would have felt the same. He made no mistake and England, despite not scoring a try, won 9–8. Was history going to repeat itself in 2005? England had not only failed to score a try, but they had never looked like creating one. Their anticipated set-piece superiority had failed to materialise, a tribute to the impact made by Ruddock on the training field. In the build-up to the game, he sent the England management into a rage by questioning the legality of the England prop Julian White's scrummaging technique. Ruddock said he would be speaking to the match referee, the New Zealander Steve Walsh, about it and asking him to make sure that the tight-head White scrummaged straight and did not bore in.

Robinson retorted by saying that there was nothing wrong with the technique of White, who in the 1990s had played for Bridgend, while Ruddock would have been aware that England had had a run-in with Walsh during the 2003 World Cup. England were playing Samoa in a group match when Walsh was the fourth official. Frustrated in their attempts to replace a player late in the match, they ended up with 16 men on the field for 30 seconds. Walsh became involved in a sideline row with Dave Reddin and allegedly squirted water from a bottle at the England fitness coach. The two men were disciplined by the tournament organisers with Walsh suspended for one match.

Walsh clearly took on board Ruddock's observation because he stood on White's side on the first few scrums when England had the put-in, but the state of the pitch was such that it was so hard for players to keep their feet that technique barely came into it. 'It felt like the earth was shaking,' said the Wales hooker Mefin Davies. 'I felt sorry for the referee. Scrums were going down because the ground was moving rather than anyone collapsing them. The turf was impossible to sidestep on. We have enough hurdles in our way without our own pitch working against us.'

The surface had been relaid two weeks before, after a hastily arranged concert that had been organised to raise money for the tsunami appeal fund. The Welsh Rugby Union reacted quickly, suspending the company responsible for maintaining the pitch, but there were some in website chatrooms who reckoned the firm's directors should have been given free debentures for ensuring that White never managed to get a foothold while Jason Robinson gave up trying to launch jinking counter-attacks from the many loose kicks which came his way because his left leg tended to go one way and his right the other, rather like Bambi on ice. It brought to mind the days when Wales would provide a bucket of dry sand for an opposition goal-kicker, and a bucket of wet stuff for their own; when it was raining, they would ensure that their hooker had a dry ball to throw into the lineout, but the opposition's hooker would be handed the equivalent of a bar of soap. Native cunning, as it were.

The turf was not a problem for Henson, who was giving the impression that he could walk on water. Stephen Jones had kicked Wales's first-half penalty, but had missed with a 48-metre effort on the hour, a kick which had looked just out of his range. Henson had come close to breaking the England defence in the 33rd minute but, surprisingly for someone so fastidious in his appearance, he had left his jersey hanging out and Tait, exacting a small measure of retribution, clutched on to it by his fingertips and a probable try was foiled. England had defended their lead with relative comfort when, as the game drifted into time added on, Robinson fielded a kick just inside his own half. Not for the first time, he slipped to the ground and was enveloped by red jerseys. The England flanker Andy Hazell entered the breakdown from the side and Walsh blew for a penalty. There was enough time for Wales to kick into the England 22 and win an attacking lineout, but their captain Gareth Thomas was mindful of what had happened against New Zealand at the Millennium Stadium a couple of months before.

On that occasion, Wales were trailing by four points in the last few minutes of the Test against Henry's and Hansen's All Blacks when they were awarded a penalty. Thomas told Henson to go for goal having looked at the stadium clock which showed that there were four minutes to play, the same clock which had confused the Springboks a fortnight earlier. Henson duly reduced the arrears to a point only for the final whistle to sound far earlier than Thomas had expected. As the Wales captain ran up to claim the ball after Walsh had awarded the penalty, Thomas looked at Stephen Jones, who shook his head. Henson stepped up.

It was the biggest decision in Thomas's short tenure as captain. He was the only player in the side who had been capped in the amateur era, making his debut in the 1995 World Cup, and, though he was winning his 81st cap and was Wales's record try scorer with 34, his career had been a chequered one. He had been used in the centre and on the wing before Hansen discovered, by accident, that he had the full-back Henry had spent so long searching for when Thomas came off the bench against New Zealand in the 2003 World Cup. Henry utilised Thomas's versatility in his last year in charge rather than considering him as the main candidate in one position and never deemed him leadership material. After Hansen had got his feet under the table, he made Thomas an integral part of his side: he appreciated the player's infectious enthusiasm and, unlike Henry, cut beneath the bluster to discover a patriot whose heart thumped loudly for his country. Though Hansen turned to another player Henry had had difficulties with, Colin Charvis, to lead the side on the 2002 tour to South Africa and beyond, he realised the galvanising effect Thomas had on the rest of the squad and he exploited his popularity. Ruddock surprised even Thomas by naming him as his first captain in October 2004: Ruddock had been expected to retain Charvis, a player he had brought to Swansea from London Welsh in 1994 as captain, but it was all about making the transition from nearly men to winners; Thomas wore his heart on his sleeve and Ruddock wanted a warrior to inspire his men. He let down Charvis gently, naming him as Thomas's vice-captain: the two players were close friends and the flanker responded with outstanding displays in the autumn series of internationals. Ruddock had pressed the right buttons.

Thomas was the only player in the Wales line-up who had tasted victory over England, as a member of the 1999 side which had won 32–31 at Wembley, another match which had been decided by a late kick, even if it was a conversion rather than a penalty. As he debated whether to let Henson take his chance, Thomas faced media criticism if Wales added another chapter to their story of glorious defeats. He had been sent to the sin-bin after 37 minutes for reacting to what he felt was an act of gratuitous foul play; as Wales mounted an attack near the England line, the Bath second row Danny Grewcock clambered over the ruck and clumsily swung his boot at the ball, connecting only with the face of the Wales scrum-half Dwayne Peel. He had committed the same offence the previous month, playing against Leinster in the Heineken Cup at the Recreation Ground when he had ended up landing a swinging foot on the Ireland scrum-half Guy

Easterby. As Peel reeled backwards, Thomas, standing 20 metres away, ran in to remonstrate with Grewcock. When he reached the breakdown, Thomas appeared to lose his balance and ended up giving Grewcock a hand-off. Walsh only took action on the recommendation of his touch judge, and the pair were shown the yellow card. 'I've been sent to my bedroom by my mother for worse,' said Thomas, 'but I was in the wrong. I should not have reacted as I did: I am the captain of the team and it is up to me to set an example. I apologised to the boys at half-time.'

Thomas did not take long to decide to tell Henson to kick Wales to glory. 'I had a word with Stephen and he said it was out of his range,' said Thomas. 'I looked at Gavin and he gave me a reassuring nod.' The crowd chanted Henson's name, recalling his record 14 conversions out of 14 against Japan at the end of November. The *Western Mail*'s 'Just Do It' exhortation boiled down to a single moment. The newspaper's headline had struck a chord: Wales were not only long overdue a victory against a country ranked in the world's top six, but England were not the team which had won the World Cup and spent the next couple of months being fêted and awarded gongs. Their head coach, Sir Clive Woodward, had resigned ten months after the World Cup triumph; instead of being a celebration of his seven years in charge, which culminated in England becoming the first northern hemisphere country to lift the Webb Ellis Trophy, his valedictory media conference turned into an undignified rant with Woodward claiming his position had been undermined by enemies within. Not even before they lost in Cardiff in 1989 and 1993 had England looked so vulnerable.

'The game was there to be lost when we went 9–8 down,' said Martyn Williams. 'The first 20 minutes had gone as we had planned, but when we failed to get two scores ahead, we became a bit edgy. We did not panic when we went behind: I suppose it was not an unusual position for us given what we had gone through in the previous couple of years, but we knew we had the chance we had been yearning for. Our season hinged on how we reacted in those final few minutes. Gavin's penalty could not have been more difficult, so far away from the posts and virtually on the touchline. I was standing next to Tom Shanklin and we both had no doubt that he would kick it.'

Some players could not bear to look. As the television cameras panned around the ground, they captured supporters with their hands clasped together in prayer. As Henson placed the ball on the ground and the noise in the stadium quickly descended from a roar to a murmur to silence, time seemed to stand still. Just Do It. And he did. And how.

CHAPTER 4

Dance by the Light of the Bridges You Burn

It's easy to be older when remembering tomorrow.

Brian Protheroe

THE LAST TIME WALES HAD FOLLOWED UP A VICTORY OVER England with success in their next championship match was back in 1988. The only true parallel for Mike Ruddock's side was 1993: in 1989 and 1999, the England fixture concluded the tournament, but 12 years ago it marked the start for Wales, who had sat out the opening round of the championship – which in those days was competed for by five nations. England had won the Grand Slam in 1991 and 1992 and, in the year of a Lions tour to New Zealand (one quirky statistic was that Wales had not lost to England in a year when the Lions were bound for the land of the long white cloud since 1930), they were fancied to become the first team to claim it three years in a row. England, led by Will

Carling, had ended a 28-year famine in Cardiff on their previous visit to the Arms Park in 1991, using their superior power up front to grind Wales into submission. They were expected to do the same again in 1993; England had a ruthlessly professional attitude even then, when the sport was still ostensibly amateur at the highest level. So, when they took the lead 9–3 in the first half, they looked to be on their way to another routine victory. Then the Wales number 8 Emyr Lewis kicked ahead into England territory. It appeared to be a futile gesture, but the Wales skipper Ieuan Evans, used to chasing lost causes in an age when he was not overwhelmed with passes, set off in pursuit. His opposite number, Rory Underwood, a colleague on the 1989 Lions tour to Australia, where they appeared together in the three Tests, seemed to have been disturbed from a deep slumber by the spectators; the crowd had started to roar on Evans and the noise served as an alarm clock to the England wing. The Welsh voices lifted Evans and by the time Underwood realised the danger, Evans was in full flight and had got to the ball. Underwood was still just breaking into his stride. Evans hacked it over the line, diving on the ball triumphantly, for Neil Jenkins to convert and put Wales into the lead.

There was no score in a tense second half, although the England scrum-half Dewi Morris felt he had touched the ball down and the full-back Jonathan Webb hit the post with a penalty. When the whistle went, it was as if Wales had won the Grand Slam. Hundreds of spectators swarmed on to the pitch, carrying off players on their shoulders, and there was a feeling of jubilation in the Welsh capital that night of the sort not generated by a rugby match since the 1970s. 'We let the victory over England go to our heads,' said the Wales outside-half that day, Neil Jenkins, in his autobiography. 'That victory over England marked one of the most satisfying moments of my career: before the match, [the

England hooker] Brian Moore had said that he could not see any way that they would lose. Statements like that have a way of coming back to haunt you. England had enough possession to win, but the beauty of the Five Nations is that it does not pay to take anything for granted.' It was only Wales's third victory in the Five Nations since they had beaten England in 1989, which perhaps explained the celebrations.

As Mike Ruddock contemplated his second match in the 2005 Six Nations, against Italy at the Stadio Flaminio in Rome, he was aware of the danger of premature celebration: Wales had ended up with the wooden spoon in 1993, and six of the side who had been involved in the victory over England had been dropped by the end of the tournament. 'There is no way we will be complacent,' said Ruddock. 'After all, Wales lost in Rome two years ago.' He made the point that there was only a week between the England and Italy internationals: in 1993, there was a fortnight interval between matches and players did not spend their time between Tests in training camps, shielded from the outside world; they had jobs to go to and could not escape the hysteria which blew up after the victory over Carling's men.

The hype after the latest victory over England surrounded Gavin Henson. Gareth Thomas had argued that the efforts of the whole team should be acknowledged rather than the spotlight fall on one man, but a player of his experience would know that few would have heard the message above the jubilant roars which echoed well into the following week, and that the media thrive on celebrity. Thomas, said the Wales team manager Alan Phillips, had told the players after the match to stay cool that evening. Henson had replied: 'You must be joking. I am a hero and people are going to expect to see me out and about.' And go out he did. 'I went into Cardiff to celebrate,' he said the following day. 'It was hard work because hordes of people were coming up to me. Our fans had stuck by us over the years and they deserved the victory.'

Graham Henry's reaction would have been to shield Henson, concerned not just that the media attention would make his head swell, but that they would turn on him the moment he had a bad game: build him up and kick him down. Ruddock was happy for Henson to front up after the match and the following day: the player had said in the build-up to the England game that he expected to be on the winning side and to contribute to the success, prompting the former Wales scrum-half Gareth Edwards to tell him in the 'Just Do It' edition of the *Western Mail* to back up his words with action.

There was a disarming honesty about Henson, which was reminiscent of the former Wales and Lions' centre Scott Gibbs, who was never concerned about what protocol demanded that he say. Gibbs spent two years with the rugby league club St Helen's in 1994; when he returned to Swansea, his first match was at Caerphilly, a one-sided romp which his side won by 50 points. Asked afterwards how he felt about his first game back, he said: 'I was bored stiff.' When he went into training the following Monday, his director of rugby, Ruddock, gave him a dressing down for undermining his colleagues, unimpressed by Gibbs's retort that he had given an honest answer to a straight question.

'I did not ask to speak to the media,' said Henson. 'The management made me do it: I am not comfortable doing all the stuff off the field, but I am really comfortable with my rugby.' It was as if Ruddock, like John Connolly when he was at Swansea, was using the media to help Henson enhance his communication skills off the field: there was no doubting his ability to express himself on it. 'Some of the players have remarked that I have grown up a lot in the three years I spent out of the Wales side,' said Henson. 'I was a bit immature before and not really ready for it. I am still shy, but now I feel that I am worth my place in the team.'

He was asked by a television interviewer what he had thought of England. The man who 24 hours before had not been fazed by the prospect of taking a difficult kick at goal in front of 74,000 spectators and a television audience numbering tens of millions smiled nervously and looked around for help before replying: 'I do not want to answer that. I will probably start slagging someone off and say something wrong. We did not play that well against England, but it was all about winning.' He was learning.

Italy had lost at home to Ireland on the opening day of the championship, a result which would have been closer had the debutant outside-half Luciano Orquera not missed three penalties in the first half. The Azzurri forwards had more than held their own in the set-pieces, and the Irish, in many eyes the favourites to win the championship, were fortunate that their captain and centre Brian O'Driscoll was at his inspirational best before leaving the field with a hamstring strain. While the beginning of a campaign had long been regarded as the best time to play France, who had a reputation for being slow starters, a reputation they were to uphold in the 2005 tournament, it was also felt that it was the worst time to take on Italy, two of whose three victories since they had entered the Six Nations in 2000 had come on the opening weekend of campaigns, against Scotland and against Wales.

If the defeat against England in August 2003 had marked Wales's nadir under Steve Hansen, the 30–22 reverse at the Stadio Flaminio 18 months before prompted a groundswell of public opinion against him: eight of the side who took the field that day – Rhys Williams, Gareth Thomas, Tom Shanklin, Dwayne Peel, Mefin Davies, Robert Sidoli, Michael Owen and Martyn Williams – were to play prominent parts in the 2005 success, while Stephen Jones was missing through injury. Iestyn Harris played at outside-half for the third, and final, time in a Wales jersey. The result was as it had been against Argentina in 2001 and against England at

Twickenham the following March, a wretched defeat; Harris had been far more effective at inside-centre where the traffic was less congested. His hesitancy in Rome proved fatal and Wales, despite having enough possession, failed to secure position and lost through tactical naivety.

A trend had emerged: Wales, like France, had become slow starters in the championship. They had not won their opening match since 1997, when they triumphed at Murrayfield, and they were becoming a soft touch away from home. Wales did rally at home in 2003, losing to England 26–9 after wasting a glorious chance to score a try on the stroke of half-time against the eventual Grand Slam winners, while Ireland, who had arrived at the Millennium Stadium having won their first three matches, were fortunate to have returned home with a victory secured by a late drop goal by their replacement outside-half Ronan O'Gara. That match demonstrated that when you are down and short of luck, decisions tend not to go your way: Wales should have been awarded a penalty, which would have won the game, when the Ireland wing Justin Bishop had appeared to have deliberately knocked the ball on in an attempt to cut out a try-scoring pass. The referee, Steve Lander of England, ruled that Bishop had been attempting to catch the ball, even though the chances of his doing so, with one hand outstretched to its full extent, appeared to have been minimal. It was another defeat, but, while the game was sandwiched between disappointing performances in Edinburgh and Paris, Wales had become competitive in Cardiff again. The previous November, they had lost to New Zealand at the Millennium Stadium, but the 43–17 scoreline distorted what had been a closely contested match until the All Blacks made their superior fitness count in the final ten minutes.

Ruddock's side had not only to cross a number of bridges but to destroy them, so that there was no going back. The victory over

DANCE BY THE LIGHT . . .

England, which had once been an almost annual event, had become a lot less frequent and therefore a cause for celebration in the Principality rather than a means to an end. Wales had not followed up a Six Nations victory with a second successive one since 2001 when they won in Paris and then Rome. Although Ruddock had named an unchanged side for Italy, he was forced to bring in the flanker Jonathan Thomas, who had made his name during the 2003 World Cup when he had made a number of clean breaks through the New Zealand defence, to replace Dafydd Jones, the Llanelli Scarlets' back rower having been ruled out by a groin injury. Much was made that season of England's injury woes, but Ruddock had had to do without the centre Sonny Parker, as well as Wales's vice-captain Colin Charvis, for the opening match. Charvis, a key figure in the autumn internationals, ended up playing no part in the Six Nations because of a foot injury while Parker, who had a neck problem, was not passed fit until the final weekend when he sat on the bench against Ireland.

The dictionary definition of serendipity is 'the making of happy and unexpected discoveries by accident or when looking for something else'. Ruddock admitted at the end of the tournament that had Charvis been fit, he would have played in the back row instead of Martyn Williams, who ended up being voted the player of the Six Nations. And Parker would probably have been preferred in the centre to Shanklin, who had been regarded by Hansen as more of a wing. When Shanklin was at Saracens in 2002, Wayne Shelford, his coach at the club, who had been the New Zealand captain when the All Blacks had trampled all over Wales in 1988, reckoned that the player, whose father Jim had been capped by Wales in the 1970s, did not have the distribution skills required for a centre and used him on the wing.

If anyone personified the new Wales, it was Shanklin. His finest hour was to come against Ireland, when he was to eclipse Brian

85

O'Driscoll, the player regarded not only as the leading outside-centre in the world, but the best for a generation. Shanklin showed against Italy that the influence of the skills coach Scott Johnson was having a telling and significant effect. He had come on as a replacement in Dublin the previous year; it would be stretching a point to say that he changed the game because Wales were trailing by 33 points, but he salvaged a sliver of respectability with two tries, breaking the Irish defence with his powerful, tackle-breaking running. By the time the 2005 tournament came around, he had allied strength with awareness, staying on his feet as a first option rather than going to ground and making a number of crucial passes. He came to look every inch an international outside-centre and the picture of O'Driscoll clad in Shanklin's jersey as the players waited for the trophy presentation ceremony to start after Wales had defeated Ireland, said more than any number of words ever could.

Shanklin had been approached by the then England head coach Clive Woodward at the start of the decade. Wales was the land of his father and Shanklin had been born in Harrow. 'Clive asked me if I would be interested in playing for England,' he said. 'It was the country where I had been born and where most of my friends were, but it was not a difficult decision to make. England were doing much better than Wales in those days, but that did not count for anything in my mind. I spoke to Francois Pienaar [the former South Africa captain who was then Saracens' chief executive] and he advised me to say yes to Clive because England's set-up was so good. They were the better team, but I wanted to play for Wales.'

He made his debut in the summer of 2001, one of Henry's last recruits. 'Things did not go well early on, but there was always a great feeling within the squad; there was no infighting or personality clashes and there were no big egos. We were all friends and that bond helped us overcome a couple of difficult years to mature into the side we are now. We know that we still have some way to go, but we turned a corner when we defeated England.'

Shanklin was very much the other centre in that match, overshadowed by Henson who hogged all the headlines. 'The opposition now see Gavin as a threat and that creates more room for players on his outside,' said Shanklin. 'Gavin's distribution skills have been overlooked with so much attention placed on his tackling and his long-range goal-kicking; he is a real team man. People get the impression that he is arrogant, but he's just Gav. It is impossible to dislike him. He takes the pressure off me because he takes so much watching. One of the strengths of the team is that we have so many players who offer a potent attacking threat; bottle up one and someone else is exploiting the space created.'

Whereas previous victories over England had prompted comparisons with past times, Ruddock's players were interested only in the tomorrow. 'Italy did very well against Ireland,' said Shanklin, three days before the Rome international. 'They have some huge forwards and they run and tackle hard. We cannot afford to take them lightly: sometimes after a great win, you take it easier in training, but we have been going flat out this week. One of the advantages of playing championship matches back-to-back, unlike the old days when there was always a fortnight's gap between them, is that you have less time to look back and dwell on what you have achieved. You have to look forward.'

Wales had gone into the Six Nations on the back of the country's worst campaign in the ten-year history of the Heineken Cup, European rugby's premier club and provincial tournament. For the first time, they had failed to produce a quarter-finalist and there were fears that the slow transition from club to regional rugby would hold back Wales for at least another couple of seasons. It was only the second year of the regional system, which had started out with five teams, four fewer than the number of clubs which had competed in the top flight of the Welsh League in the 2002–03 season. Celtic Warriors had been disbanded in the summer of 2004 after their owner, Leighton Samuel, had sold his share to the Welsh Rugby Union, which had originally wanted four regions, settling for five after being threatened with legal action by clubs who, five years before, had signed ten-year agreements guaranteeing them income if they remained in the top division. Two of the original five regions were made up of single clubs, Llanelli and Cardiff. Neath and Swansea combined to form the Ospreys, the Warriors were an alliance between Bridgend and Pontypridd while Newport and Ebbw Vale formed the Gwent Dragons, who were coached by Ruddock.

The first year of regional rugby coincided with the World Cup. Llanelli Scarlets won the Celtic League and were the only one of the five to make the last eight of the Heineken Cup, although they were knocked out in the quarter-finals, despite having home advantage against Biarritz. Llanelli had flown the Welsh flag in Europe since the start of the new millennium, but by the start of the 2004–05 season the Scarlets were in the throes of transition and had lost their playmaker, Stephen Jones, to Clermont Auvergne. The Dragons had replaced Ruddock with Chris Anderson, a former Australia rugby league coach, who had no previous experience of the 15-a-side code, while Cardiff Blues had started as Cardiff had finished the club era, also-rans rather than pacesetters. The fusion of Neath and Swansea, who as clubs had both flirted with financial ruin, proved the most harmonious: Ebbw Vale and Newport quickly fell out and the region became known as Newport Gwent Dragons, while the Warriors, before they ceased to exist, had alienated supporters in the Rhondda Valley by establishing Bridgend's Brewery Field ground as its base, all but ignoring Pontypridd's Sardis Road.

Ruddock had gone into the November internationals on the back of a poor start to the Heineken Cup by the four regions, with seven matches out of eight ending in defeat. All the battles with French and English clubs had been lost, with the solitary success recorded by the Dragons, who had defeated Edinburgh at a deserted Murrayfield. With Hansen not receiving public recognition for the way he had developed the national squad, it was not surprising that the popular view was that Wales would struggle until the regional system had settled down. That analysis failed to appreciate that the national side was much further down the development road than the regions, as Wales were to show by pushing both South Africa and New Zealand all the way in November 2004.

Hansen had driven the regional idea, which had been championed by Henry, who, very soon after arriving in Wales, despaired at what he saw as the flabby side of professional rugby, where, when players talked about performance, they were often referring to their cars rather than the rugby field. 'There are too many professional teams,' he said before the 1999 World Cup. 'Talent is being spread too thinly around and players are not having to fight for their places enough. The gap between club and international rugby is too large: there is only enough money and talent in Wales to sustain four sides, in my view. New Zealand, a country with only a slightly larger population than Wales, has five Super 12 sides. Players here are in a comfort zone and need to be jerked out of it.'

The clubs did not relinquish their status without a sustained and, at times, farcical fight, but they accepted that having nine professional teams was not feasible financially. On average, they received less than £1 million each from central funds, while only Newport had a commercial arm to rival those of the leading

English clubs. The club game, which had underpinned Welsh rugby since the 1870s, was dying. David Moffett, a hard-nosed Englishman, who had spent most of his working life in Australia and New Zealand, had been brought in as the WRU's chief executive to help reduce the considerable debt built up by the governing body. It was clear that financial success would only be driven by a winning national side and Moffett, armed with more power and authority than his predecessors, who had quaintly been called secretaries, drove a hard bargain. He eventually got his way, but when the Warriors collapsed the four regions stretched from east to west along the M4 belt.

'The teams of the last golden era were rooted in a way this one is not,' said the co-author of the official history of the WRU, David Smith, before the final match of the 2005 Six Nations against Ireland. 'In the 1970s, they could tap into succeeding generations of talent: you lose Barry John, you find Phil Bennett. My fear now is that it will not be so easy in the future, because of the way rugby has been destroyed north of the M4.' When the WRU closed the Warriors in the summer of 2004, supporters in Bridgend and Pontypridd urged a boycott of internationals at the Millennium Stadium. When Wales played South Africa that November, the attendance was the lowest at the ground for an international against a major southern hemisphere nation, more than 20,000 short of its 74,000 capacity. Moffett, following the lead of the Australian Rugby Union in the 2003 World Cup, had sold tickets for the Tests against the Springboks and New Zealand in conjunction with Wales's other two internationals that month against the considerably inferior draws of Romania and Japan. The antagonism directed at him at the beginning of the month had faded by the end, a result of the inspiring performances by Wales against South Africa and the All Blacks, and the kick-off for the final match of the quartet, against the Japanese, had to be delayed because of the queues of spectators trying to get into the ground.

So, in 2005, as Wales flew to Rome, opinion was divided about whether the victory over England marked a new beginning or signified another dead-end. Italy were quietly confident: their coach John Kirwan, who had been part of the 1988 New Zealand side which had destroyed Wales, fancied his side's chances at forward. He warned about the dangers of Ruddock's men on the counter-attack, and as the match failed to go the way he had hoped, he was caught on camera with a look of disgust when his backs had hoofed the ball aimlessly to Wales's back three and paid the ultimate price. If Henson had been the story the week before, in Rome it was a case of Just Williams: Shane, on the left wing, and Martyn at wing forward, gladiators who put Roman noses firmly out of joint.

Shane Williams had provided Hansen with the Kiwi's moment of serendipity in the 2003 World Cup. After making an eye-catching start to his international career in the 2000 Six Nations, scoring a try on his first full appearance against Italy in Cardiff, he looked to have been caught in the dying embers of Henry's reign. He played in the side which had lost 36–6 at home to Ireland in the rearranged championship match in 2001, but then disappeared back into club rugby. As the World Cup loomed, he had not made any of Hansen's squads and was not regarded as being in contention for Australia. He played in the friendly against Romania in August 2003 in a team which was largely made up of Wales's second tier of players, sandwiched as it was between the warm-ups against England and Scotland. Williams scored two tries and caused havoc with his jinking feet.

'I was driving to training with the Ospreys a week or so later when my phone rang,' said Williams. 'It was Steve Hansen telling me that I was in the World Cup squad. I thought it was one of my teammates winding me up and laughed it off. It took me a few minutes to realise the call was genuine and I had to get on to the other side of the M4 and drive to Wales's base in the Vale of Glamorgan. To say it was a shock was an understatement: I had been nowhere near the squad, and quite rightly so because a run of injuries had left me struggling for form. To this day, I do not know why Steve chose me. I had not given up hope of an international recall, but things had happened so fast for me – I went from being a nobody to someone whose face was on advertising hoardings and back again – that you learn not to expect. Graham Henry had tried to protect me when I first rose to prominence: he took me under his wing and I will always be grateful to him.'

Williams was named in the World Cup squad as a third scrum-half, though he was not involved in the opening trio of pool matches, against Canada, Tonga and Italy. But when Wales played New Zealand in their final World Cup match, with a place in the quarter-finals already assured, Hansen mixed up the side and Williams was chosen on the wing more than two years after he had lined up against Ireland. 'I knew it could be my last chance on an international field,' he said. 'I was determined to make the most of it and it was one of those lovely days when things happened for me.' Williams captured the imagination of the Australian public, who until then had regarded the World Cup as an over-hyped bore: one of the smallest figures on the field, he left a trail of destruction behind him as he stepped in and out of tackles with the mesmeric quality of a George Best, re-emphasising that rugby union was a game for all shapes and sizes after a period when it had appeared in danger of becoming almost indistinguishable from rugby league, where positional individuality had become homogenised.

Shane Williams's try in Rome in 2005 summed up not only Wales's burgeoning confidence, but also showed how they were widening the boundaries of the game by keeping the ball alive in the tackle and seeking space rather than contact. The following day at Twickenham was to provide a contrast when France won 18–17 despite failing to produce a single handling move of note, prevailing with six kicks from the boot of Dimitri Yachvili, but freedom of expression only flourished at the Stadio Flaminio.

Wales had already scored four tries when Gareth Thomas and Martyn Williams combined to put away Kevin Morgan, who had come on as a replacement for the wing Hal Luscombe. Morgan was tackled to the ground but, in the act of falling, managed to swivel his body so that he was able to flick a pass to Shane Williams and there was no stopping the Ospreys wing, who exploded onto the ball at pace before running in the try.

Shane Williams was involved in four of his side's six tries – two of which were scored by the outstanding second row pairing of Brent Cockbain and Robert Sidoli – while his namesake Martyn got a crucial score just before the interval when he had the presence of mind to ground the ball on the base of a goal-post having been tackled just short of the line. It gave Wales a 19–5 lead at the interval. The half had for the most part been an even contest, but Italy, as they had against Ireland the previous week, failed to turn penalties into points with the full-back Roland de Marigny missing three kicks in the opening minutes. Orquera had been relieved of the goal-kicking load, but scored his side's try after catching Henson's attempted kick-ahead and running 55 metres to the line. The Azzurri created little, and while Stephen Jones remarked afterwards that Wales had played total rugby at times, in the way the great Holland sides of the 1970s had played total football, what was also evident was that while Wales had flair to burn, they also had a defence which took some breaking down: one interception try in two matches vindicated Ruddock's decision to recall Clive Griffiths, who had been released by

Hansen after a clash of personalities, as the defence coach.

Kirwan's response was to tip Wales for the title. 'They are championship material, without any doubt,' he said. 'They are a lot more confident in what they are doing than they were even a year ago and the win over England has clearly bolstered their belief. If you give them space, they can be outstanding and we made the mistake of putting in too many loose kicks. When you have guys like Shane Williams running the ball back at you from deep, you have to watch out.' Shane Williams summed up his side's mood: 'We came into this game knowing that we did not want to be the squad that beat England but lost the following week,' he said. His use of the word squad, rather than team, was significant: it was something constantly emphasised by Hansen. Wales were a 22, not a 15; even if a replacement did not make it on to the field, his work in the build-up to a match deserved to be recognised.

It was the first time that Wales had won their opening two matches in a championship since 1994, the last occasion when they had clinched the title. It was also their first away victory in the Six Nations for four years, but Ruddock and his squad refused to talk about the past. 'I do not know if teams will fear us now, but they will certainly respect us,' said Stephen Jones. 'It is not just that we are playing a great style of rugby, but we are an experienced squad, one which has got to this position because of the hard work we have put in and the hard times we have gone through.'

Ruddock insisted: 'We are not talking about the Triple Crown, the Grand Slam or the title. All we are concentrating on is our next match, France in Paris. We have not played to our maximum potential yet. I am quietly confident that we can get a positive result in France, but we are going to have to improve our game to achieve that.' His words showed how there had been a sea-change from the recent past: Henry always played down Wales's prospects, even when they were on their ten-match winning streak under him, preferring to talk up the opposition and paint his team as underdogs. He felt that the players were too fragile mentally to cope with the weighty burden of expectation; while there was little in the way of expectation or optimism during Hansen's two years in charge, he changed the mind-set of the players. One of the differences that Ruddock made was that he saw there was nothing to be gained by playing down the ability of his squad: after every match he gave them another gentle nudge in the right direction.

It was all about tomorrow. As you crossed one bridge and burned it, you did not look back. It was left to the Wales supporters, daring to believe for the first time in six years, to frolic in the afterglow.

CHAPTER 5

Running Man

Hurry up time, speed us away.

Jen Chapin

CLASSIC MATCHES INVARIABLY CONTAIN ONE MOMENT which imprints itself in the mind's eye, and as a result of that the game is indelibly etched on the memory: there was Phil Bennett's seemingly suicidal series of sidesteps near his own line when playing for the Barbarians against New Zealand at Cardiff Arms Park in 1973, the start of what was to become rugby's most celebrated try, scored by Gareth Edwards with a flourishing dive in the left-hand corner, 100 metres from where Bennett had picked up the ball; Keith Jarrett's burst along the Arms Park touchline in Wales's 1967 victory over England in Cardiff; John Taylor's last-minute touchline conversion to win Wales's 1971 international against Scotland at Murrayfield; the shoulder charge by J.P.R. Williams which prevented Jean-Francois Gourdon from scoring a try for France which would have denied Wales the

GRAND SLAM!

Grand Slam at Cardiff in 1976; the Australia second row Justin Harrison's lineout steal from Martin Johnson to deny the Lions their last chance to win the 2001 series; Jonny Wilkinson's late, late drop goal in the 2003 World Cup final; Paul Ringer's dismissal at Twickenham in 1980; and, in late February 2005, when Paris shivered in the snow, the Wales outside-half Stephen Jones sidestepped out of the shadows of his illustrious predecessors with a scintillating break that was to change the course of that season's Six Nations campaign.

Lost in the debate about the merits of returning to a Welsh coach in Mike Ruddock after six years when New Zealanders had been in charge, was the fact that not only had Ruddock himself broadened his outlook by spending three years in charge of the Irish province Leinster from 1997, having spent a season at the start of the decade as the coach of a Dublin club, Bective Rangers, but also the fact that Jones was one of two players currently playing in France. When Gareth Thomas arrived for the toss of the coin before Wales's third match of the 2005 championship at the Stade de France, waiting for him to call wrongly was his club captain at Toulouse, the second row Fabien Pelous, the France skipper. Those who maintained that Graham Henry and Steve Hansen, Ruddock's immediate two predecessors, had set back the course of the Welsh game by bringing a southern hemisphere approach to the national squad ignored the fact that Ruddock, who had been put in charge of Ireland A and had helped out at some of the national side's training sessions, had also been a cross-pollinator. Long before the game turned professional in 1995, coaches from the south joined clubs in Britain and Ireland: just as Ruddock had turned Swansea from flops to the tops in the space of a year in the 1991–92 season, so the Australian Alex Evans was the following year to transform Cardiff from a laughing stock into, eventually, champions. Evans was Wales's caretaker coach during the 1995 World Cup, assisted by Ruddock; like many before, and after, him he wondered why the natural talent of young Welsh players rarely turned into fulfilment at international level.

Evans could not understand players who wasted their abilities through a lack of effort and the players he had most impact with – the hooker Jonathan Humphreys (a future Wales captain) and the second row Derwyn Jones – two club journeymen before the arrival of the Australian, were receptive to Evans's ideas. The fact that he was from a country 12,000 miles away had nothing to do with it: it was what he had to say, not the accent in which he said it. When Hansen followed Henry back to New Zealand in the summer of 2004 to join him in the All Blacks' management team, the Welsh Rugby Union chief executive, David Moffett, jokingly suggested that the New Zealand Rugby Union should pay compensation to Wales for developing the pair as coaches. Ireland could have said the same when Ruddock left to return to Wales in 2000, though their national side at the time was being coached by a New Zealander, Warren Gatland. In fact, all four home unions have had coaches from the southern hemisphere on their management teams in the last eight years. When New Zealand lost the 1971 Test series to the Lions, they immediately sent a delegation of coaches to the British Isles to find out what had been going on; when Australia sank to their lowest ever ebb in 1973 after losing to Tonga in Brisbane, they sent for Ray Williams, then the WRU's coaching organiser, who had been in the vanguard of the first coaching revolution in the 1960s.

Stephen Jones had left Llanelli Scarlets for Clermont Auvergne, the formerly named Montferrand, in the summer of 2004. He had joined Llanelli as an 18 year old and had spent his senior career with the club, living all his life in west Wales. He was one of the few players in the 2005 squad to have won his first cap in the pre-Henry era, having come on as a replacement during the 96–13 defeat to South Africa in Pretoria in 1998. Jones, who was given his first international start by Henry during the 2000 Six Nations, was regarded as the natural successor to Neil Jenkins, Wales's outside-half for most of the 1990s who, when he retired from Test rugby in 2002, had accumulated more points than any other player in the history of the international game, 1,090, and had won more Wales caps than anyone else, 87. Despite his success, Jenkins was not universally accepted by Welsh supporters; he did not fit the romantic image of Welsh outside-halfs. He did not ghost through defenders like Barry John, sidestep like Bennett or possess the acceleration or cheek of Jonathan Davies. He was more prosaic but, in his own way, equally effective. As rugby had evolved, outside-halfs could no longer regard tackling as an optional extra. Before a battered shoulder afflicted him in the last couple of years of his career, Jenkins was one of the hardest tackling outside-halfs the game had seen, an attribute also possessed by Stephen Jones.

For most of his career, Jenkins did not have the luxury of a dominant pack, invariably finding himself forced to live off scraps of possession. It was the same for Jones in 2003 and 2004, but at club, and then regional, level he was a key figure at Llanelli, an all-round tactician who looked more assertive there than he did on the international field. By the end of the 2003–04 season, he was 27. The Scarlets wanted him to sign a new contract which would have taken him into his 30s. If he was going to leave Wales and experience a new environment, this was his last chance. Leicester, the dominant club in England and in Europe for most of the decade, saw him as the answer to a long-term problem at outside-half. Jones went to the club's Welford Road ground and was taken out by a group of players; even when Montferrand moved in, it was felt he would join the Tigers rather than a French club which was renowned for its political instability. Before he made his decision, though, Jones spoke at length to the Wales skills coach Scott Johnson. Leicester were turned down and he signed for Clermont, who shortly afterwards blew the final of the Parker Pen Challenge Cup against Harlequins in Reading, and with it a guaranteed place in the following season's Heineken Cup, by acts of rank indiscipline when they all but had the game won.

'I had reached a point in my career where I felt that I needed a change – not just as a rugby player, but as a person,' said Jones. 'I had spent all my life in one country and all my career at the same club. I knew that moving to France would be different in so many ways, including the language. When I first arrived, I did wonder whether I had made the right move: the club's international players, whom I knew, were not back from their break and everyone else was a stranger to me. No one spoke English and my French was worse. It was like moving to a new school. I struggled to adapt to the French game at first: we had a poor start to the season and were stuck in the relegation zone for a while, but things quickly changed for the better.'

It was fitting, if a touch ironic, given the fundamental change he had undergone at Clermont, that Jones's apotheosis as an international outside-half should come at France's national stadium. 'British rugby is a lot more structured than the French game,' he said. 'In France, they play more off-the-cuff, with their heads up, and you react to what is in front of you. Wales had evolved a style of play under Steve Hansen which relied less on structure and Mike Ruddock took it on. We play at a quick tempo and have forwards who are capable of reacting quickly to situations. What is most significant is that we are a young squad: virtually all the players will be around in the 2007 World Cup. When you look back at the 2003 World Cup quarter-final against England, none of our back row that day – Colin Charvis, Dafydd

Jones and Jonathan Thomas – was in the starting line-up against France: we are starting to develop strength in depth and youngsters are coming into a winning environment.'

Jonathan Thomas, despite scoring the opening try in Rome, was left out of the side for Paris, with Ruddock not afraid to change a winning combination. The bulkier Ryan Jones was brought in to offer a more physical presence at the breakdown; he was the only player who started a match in the 2005 Six Nations who had not been involved in the Hansen era. It was two weeks before his 24th birthday and he had been playing rugby for fewer than seven years. 'At the start of the season, playing for Wales was the last thing on my mind,' said Ryan Jones, who had made his debut against South Africa the previous November. 'I had set my sights on cementing my place in the Neath-Swansea Ospreys' back row and being involved in the Heineken Cup. It has been a whirlwind experience.' Jones had been a replacement against England and his inclusion meant that Ruddock had used three blind-side flankers in as many matches.

Whereas Ruddock had made one voluntary change to a winning team, his opposite number in France, Bernard Laporte, had made three. Like Wales, France had a 100 per cent record after the opening two rounds, but their 16–9 victory over Scotland in Paris on the first weekend had been ill-deserved; 9–0 down at one stage against a side regarded as the weakest in the tournament, they had won thanks to a late try from a charged down clearance. The Scotland coach Matt Williams raged that his side had had a legitimate try disallowed, a view left not proven by television replays, and that a late yellow card had been unwarranted. If the club game Stephen Jones had become used to encouraged players to look up, Laporte's team played with their heads down, and not even France's first victory at Twickenham since 1997 satisfied their rugby public. If the French had lacked ambition against the Scots, they were one-dimensional against England, winning 18–17 despite not once threatening to score a try. They had trailed 17–6 at the interval before mounting an unlikely comeback, just as Wales in Paris were to go into the break 15–6 down having been completely outplayed.

'All we said to the players was that they had to stop giving away penalties,' said the France defence coach Dave Ellis. 'England had scored two tries because we had missed tackles, but they had not looked really threatening. We told the players to let them have the ball, and once we had sorted out our defence, England did not make any inroads. We put them under pressure and they gave away penalties.' The England head coach Andy Robinson complained afterwards that France hardly merited their success, having shown no creative desire, but England had not apologised in 1999 when they had beaten France at Twickenham thanks to Jonny Wilkinson's seven penalties, with the French scoring the only try of the match. It was only England's second defeat at home in the championship for seven years, but Laporte could not have been under more pressure had his side lost their opening two matches.

Laporte, as he had done in 2003, went into the Six Nations insisting that he had his sights on the World Cup, which France were hosting in 2007, rather than the championship. He said he was going to use the next couple of months to look at players and combinations, but even though he had a long-term contract, he was forced to reconsider the direction in which he was taking his side after an onslaught in the French media against what was seen as a style of play more typical of England than France. He recalled the powerful wing Aurelien Rougerie, giving him orders to impose himself physically on Shane Williams, and he gave a first cap to the flanker Yannick Nyanga, having opted for a back row against England which had contained a number 8 on the open-side in Sebastien Chabal. Yannick Jauzion returned to the centre in place of Brian Liebenberg and Julien Laharrague, who had played most of his rugby on the wing for Brive, made his debut at full-back. The back division brimmed with attacking intent, even if Laporte had retained Yann Delaigue at outside-half, resisting calls to bring the more mercurial Frederic Michalak off the bench.

Some Wales players hinted after the victory that they had gone into the game with an element of complacency, not believing that France would radically change their style and that the afternoon would offer a contrast in styles between France's set-piece prowess, backed up by driving mauls, and Wales's counter-attacking style. Within five minutes, any notions of a Parisian cakewalk had been rudely shattered. The France of the previous couple of weeks had been shunted into the sidings, replaced by something far sleeker and faster. In the opening half, France produced the best rugby seen in the tournament not just in 2005 but for several years, superior even to Wales's first-half demolition of Scotland the following month. It was like watching the France of old with players queuing up to handle the ball, but it was not unstructured. Ellis, who doubled up as Gloucester's defence coach and had helped out in some Ospreys' training sessions, had identified a defensive weakness in the Wales three-quarter line: while Henson's front-on tackling was brutally uncompromising, he was less effective taking out attackers side on. Ellis also believed that Shane Williams, for all his attacking threat, was a weak link defensively.

If Wales had believed that France would be unable to play at a sufficiently high tempo, they were forced to think again. Four minutes had elapsed when the scrum-half Dimitri Yachvili caught the prop Gethin Jenkins out of position and flashed over for a try. Rougerie had set up the breakdown with a barging run, and within eight minutes France had added their second try. Delaigue went outside Henson, though the New Zealand referee Paul Honiss missed a trip on the Wales centre by the France flanker Serge Betsen, who many argued should not have been playing in the Six Nations, having escaped disciplinary action for a trip on the England centre Stuart Abbott during Biarritz's Heineken Cup victory over Wasps, an act which had left Abbott with a broken leg and a prematurely concluded season. His sleight-of-foot on Henson was missed by the officials, not surprisingly because Betsen put his foot out while looking the other way, and it was impossible to tell after several television replays what his intent was. He protested his innocence afterwards, but Henson was left sitting on the floor without one of his silver boots as Delaigue exploited the space the Wales centre had vacated and Rougerie finished off in the corner.

As the Wales players gathered under the posts for Yachvili's conversion, they had returned to a place they hoped they had left behind. Steve Hansen was watching the match on television in the early hours of a New Zealand Sunday morning, detached yet bound to the players he had nurtured. 'I thought back to our game against the All Blacks at Waikato in 2003,' he said. 'We lost 55–3 having been outplayed all over the park and we realised then that we had to step up our effort in training. I knew that the guys would not panic in Paris because they had a confidence they did not possess a couple of years before, the knowledge that they could live with the best teams in the world. It was clear against England and Italy that the belief was there, and it was just a matter of hanging in there and waiting for their moment. I did not think that the game was over at half-time: it was precisely because of what the players had been through, having to learn from the pain of defeat, that they had developed a harder edge.'

Wales, somehow, did not concede another try in the first half. The centre Damien Traille thought he had scored, but was called back for a foot in touch; Rougerie was a threat every time he had the ball, charging at Shane Williams like a bull at a matador; Laharrague injected pace from full-back, while Delaigue, who had been hesitant at Twickenham, was a revelation. While Wales were fêted at the end of the tournament for their free-running rugby, it was their defence in the final 25 minutes of the first half and in the last ten minutes of the second period which delivered victory in Paris as much as Martyn Williams's two second-half tries. Under intense pressure in the scrums and in the lineout, Wales not only kept their shape defensively but, vitally, maintained their discipline. They conceded only five penalties in the whole match, a remarkable statistic for a team playing away from home, never mind one which had spent three-quarters of the afternoon on the back foot. France, in contrast, wasted some promising positions by giving away penalties at the breakdown, and Wales went into the interval partially reinvigorated by Stephen Jones's second penalty which left them with a single-figure deficit, despite having spent almost the entire half mobilised in defence.

Ruddock was asked at the end of the match what he had said to his side at half-time. If the questioner expected the answer to reveal a Churchillian exhortation to the players to go out there and do it for their country, or the Sir Alex Ferguson hair-dryer treatment, he was to be disappointed. 'I did not say much at all,' revealed Ruddock. 'I did not think I had to. I just focused on turnovers, tackles and touch: we had conceded turnovers and missed tackles and kicks to touch. We had to redouble our efforts: nine points did not add up to a big gap. France had had a great first half, partly because of the errors we had made. We were only two scores away and the next 40 minutes were going to tell us everything about the mental strength of the players, a strength which showed through in the final few minutes when the French were throwing everything they had at us.'

It was the Wales second row Brent Cockbain's first international in Paris. An Australian who had been brought into the squad in 2003 by Hansen after he had qualified for Wales on residential grounds, having joined Pontypridd from London Irish in 1999, Cockbain's brother, Matt, had been a member of the Wallabies' World Cup squad in 1999 and 2003. Brent Cockbain stood at 6 ft 8 in. tall and weighed more than 18 st., and Hansen, when asked why he had turned to a player from the southern hemisphere when the eligibility scandal of 2000 was still fresh in the memory, replied: 'Because we do not grow players of his size in Wales. He is also aggressive and does not take any messing about. He is qualified to play for us and I would be stupid not to take advantage.'

Cockbain had played in four of Wales's five World Cup matches in 2003 and had scored his first international try in the 2005 Six Nations victory in Rome, taking the ball 25 metres from the posts and swerving out of a tackle before galloping to the line. If he had been seen before as a one-dimensional front five forward, at his happiest when plastered in elbow grease, he showed at the Stadio Flaminio that there was another side to his game. Had there been an award for the most improved player of the tournament that year, Cockbain would have been among the leading candidates, along with Tom Shanklin and Gethin Jenkins. The trio personified how Wales had grown as a side since the end of the 2004 championship, and were not afraid to show off the full range of their talents.

'We showed against Italy, when four of the six tries were scored by forwards, that every player from 1 to 15 could handle the ball and off-load,' said Cockbain. 'The credit for that is down to Steve Hansen, Scott Johnson and Mike Ruddock. They have spent hours with us on the training field helping us to perfect the skills. It is high-risk rugby, but it is exciting as a player to be a part of it. It stimulates you and there is a lot more to come from us. The key moment in the 2005 Six Nations for me was the half-time interval in Paris: we had come through a storm, but we had not capsized. When we sat down in the dressing-room, Mike did not say anything at first: he waited for us to relax and he talked us through a few things which needed improving. There was no panic. We knew what we had to do.'

France started the second half as they had finished the first, running at the heart of the Welsh defence. Less than a minute had gone by when, 20 metres from their own line, Wales turned over French possession, Ruddock's words having an immediate effect. The ball was quickly passed to Stephen Jones who, everyone expected, would hoof the ball into touch. A year before, he would probably have done so but, as he had become used to at Clermont Auvergne, he lifted his head up after receiving the ball and immediately realised that the French defence was fragmented. For all their traditional flair, élan and ability to improvise with the ball in hand, the French have a tendency to be slow to react in defence when taken by surprise. Jones's predecessor, Neil Jenkins, had stunned France at the same ground in the 1999 Five Nations when he had received the kick-off in his own 22 and, instead of kicking for touch as everyone had expected, had set off on a darting run, lighting the touch-paper for an astonishing 40 minutes of rugby which even left those watching short of breath. One commentator remarked afterwards that after watching Jones keep the ball in his hands and shimmy through a gap, he was reminded of Barry John. It was probably the first time anyone had made the comparison, but Jones did as John often had done, and kept on running.

'I had a big advantage when I had the ball,' Barry John once said. 'I knew what I was going to do: my opponents could only guess. That knowledge gave me an edge I knew I would be able to exploit, even if I had to wait 60 or 70 minutes.' As he set off on his run which was to take him 50 metres up the field, Stephen Jones admitted afterwards that he was not quite sure he was doing the right thing. 'My teammates asked me what I was up to: it was a good question and I did not know the answer myself. I was just looking for someone to come up on my shoulder quickly and when that did not happen I kept going. The French defenders seemed to be thinking that I was going to offload the ball any second and they hung off me. I ran on and waited for the support to arrive.'

It eventually did in the form of the Williamses, Martyn and Shane, and the former ended up scoring in the left-hand corner after a bout of interpassing which had seen Shane exact a measure of retribution on Rougerie, Jones's Clermont clubmate, by sprinting past him.

France, from having the chance to go a potentially match-winning 22–6 ahead, had conceded the type of try they were renowned for scoring. It was like a boxer who, having absorbed blows which should have finished him off, clambers off the ropes to deliver a punch which, as much through surprise as pain, disorientates his opponent who, by the time he manages to clear his head, finds that a contest he was running away with has become a real scrap. France were still reeling a couple of minutes later when Martyn Williams took a quick penalty just a few metres from the French line and, as he had done in Rome, showed great presence of mind at the moment of reckoning by stretching his left hand out at an angle and away from the last defender, straining every sinew to ensure that he touched the ball down on the line.

As transformations go, it resembled not so much France's comeback at Twickenham two weeks before, which had been a gradual accretion of points through Yachvili's boot, as their 1999 World Cup semi-final against New Zealand at Twickenham. The

GRAND SLAM!

All Blacks had gone 24–10 ahead that afternoon after their giant wing Jonah Lomu had scored a try early in the second half and their supporters had their minds set on an appearance in the following Saturday's final against their arch-rivals Australia at the Millennium Stadium. Lomu's emergence in the 1995 World Cup, when he had trampled through defences, had led to a school of thought which stressed that big was beautiful. Forget grace and style, when you had a 20-stone wing coming towards you like an out-of-control dump truck, who needed a Gerald Davies? Shane Williams was to make his Wales debut two months after France's World Cup semi-final, by which time the wing Christophe Dominici, still in the side in 2005, had pulled the rug out from underneath the stampeding Lomu's feet. Dominici's try in the 1999 semi-final gave France the lead after Christophe Lamaison had softened up the All Blacks with four kicks; by the time New Zealand had regathered their wits, they had conceded 33 points without reply and another World Cup campaign had ended in tears for them.

As Martyn Williams celebrated his second try, France started to panic. Laporte had been shrewd in his use of substitutions at Twickenham, bringing on the front rowers Olivier Milloud and William Servat to make an impact on the hour, the point at which France were growing stronger as England wilted; Servat came on against Wales after Williams's first try with Milloud quickly following. Delaigue was also taken off prematurely and France lost direction. They had gone behind without doing much wrong and little needed fixing. Laporte spoke at the end of the championship about a 'mad ten minutes at the second half against Wales which cost us a second successive Grand Slam', but he himself had been part of the madness. By the time France got their heads around what had happened, they were 24–18 behind with Stephen Jones kicking a penalty and dropping a goal after

Michalak had potted one for France.

The last ten minutes were all France. They laid siege to the Wales line, but every time they worked an opening it was quickly closed. 'I was not wholly confident that we could hold on,' said Stephen Jones. 'France are superb when they are looking to play, probably the best team in the world. I was pleased when my drop goal went over because it meant that France had to score a try and convert it to win the match. We had to keep them away from the middle of the pitch and out wide. It was all hands on deck and it got tense when they had a series of attacking scrums at the very end. We gave away a few penalties and there was always the fear that we would concede a penalty try and lose the match by a point, but our defence was outstanding and a lot of credit had to go to our defence coach, Clive Griffiths.'

The end eventually came after a French scrum had come to grief when the replacement number 8 Imanol Harinordoquy lost control and Wales took charge of the ball. The Frenchman was to pay for his blemish by being dropped from the squad for the following match against Ireland in Dublin, and was ungracious in defeat afterwards, saying that he had not been particularly impressed with Wales's defence which, he contended, would be vulnerable against a side which combined an ability to win ball with the prowess to hold on to it.

It was fitting that the last player to handle the ball was Stephen Jones. When he received a pass inside his in-goal area, he had been told by the referee that the next time the ball went out of play would signal the end of the game. Instead of kicking the ball into touch, Jones turned away from his teammates and thumped it over the dead-ball line. He had not wanted to risk missing touch and giving the elusive Dominici the chance to run at Wales for a final time, but, as the Welsh supporters in the crowd held their voices, not knowing whether to shout or keep biting their fingernails,

GRAND SLAM!

Honiss did not put his whistle in his mouth straight away. Jones suddenly feared he had given France an attacking five-metre scrum instead of Wales victory, reminiscent of Neil Jenkins with the Lions in South Africa at the end of the second Test in Durban. The French referee Didier Mene had told Jenkins that the next time the ball went out of play, he would blow the final whistle. On that day, the Lions were leading 18–15 and were already 1–0 up in the three-Test series. Jenkins had a 22-metre drop-out and, urged on by his colleagues, kicked the ball high into the stand. Mene, perhaps motivated by mischief, did not blow immediately, and it was the same with Honiss in Paris. 'When I kicked the ball dead, I had a horrible thought that the referee had found some extra seconds to add on,' said Stephen Jones. 'I looked at him, he looked back at me and I could see some of the players glancing in my direction, wondering if I had got it wrong. It seemed a lifetime before the ref finally blew the whistle and we could celebrate. It was a huge victory, one which was even more important than the success against England. A number of the players had been in the Wales squad which was whitewashed in the Six Nations two seasons before; the team spirit we showed at the end, when everyone worked for each other as France threw everything they had at us, was born out of the adversity we had endured.'

Wales had defeated England and France in the same championship season for only the second time since they had won the Grand Slam in 1978: the other occasion had been in 1999, under Graham Henry, when, after losing their opening two matches to Scotland and Ireland and being rated odds-on to clinch another whitewash and wooden spoon, they gave the French an eyeful in Paris and waltzed down Wembley Way having handed off England. In 2005, the nearly men had taken their biggest step on their way to becoming history men, but Ruddock and his players had refused to talk about the Grand Slam, even though the increasingly feeble Scots, who had followed up their heartening opener in Paris by collapsing against Ireland at Murrayfield, were next up in Edinburgh.

'We cannot afford to get ahead of ourselves,' said Ruddock. 'Scotland will have nothing to lose and they will throw everything at us. We have belief and confidence now and have picked up two victories away from home which both showed the mental strength of the players.' After the end of the tournament, he said he had deliberately played down talk of the Grand Slam. 'It would have put more pressure on the players. The danger was that they would start thinking in terms of that or the Six Nations title rather than the next game itself and the plan we wanted to implement. I think our approach allowed the players to play with the freedom we had asked of them: at no point were they afraid to go out and express themselves.' Cockbain took up the theme, saying: 'France had the chances to beat us and we made them pay,' he said. 'A bounce of the ball or a referee's decision could have meant the end of our unbeaten record; we have to go to Scotland with all guns blazing and play our own game. People seem to be getting ahead of themselves by talking about our final match against Ireland, but we have to keep pushing ourselves. Murrayfield will be our biggest test so far.'

The victory at the Stade de France was achieved at a cost. Gareth Thomas had to be replaced at half-time after breaking his right thumb in five places and would play no further part in the championship. As Ruddock's first captain and the heartbeat of his side, Thomas would have to be replaced as a motivator as well as a player. Ruddock, shrewdly, asked Thomas to remain with the squad for the final two weeks of the campaign while the captaincy passed to the number 8 Michael Owen, a less voluble character than Thomas and an astute thinker. Leadership, which had been identified by Graham Henry four years previously as a problem, was no longer an issue. Hansen had been ridiculed for naming five captains when Wales toured South Africa in the summer of 2002, but it was his way of making players, some of whom could no longer be called inexperienced, assume some responsibility. In the 2005 side, Martyn Williams, Stephen Jones and Owen had captaincy experience at international level, while the replacement hooker Robin McBryde had been one of Hansen's five captains.

Thomas, Wales's first player to be plastered in Paris that day when his broken thumb was put in a protective cast, struck a typically upbeat note afterwards, pointing out the quality of the player who had replaced him at the Stade de France, Rhys Williams. Whereas in past years, attention would have been lavished on an injury suffered by a Wales captain, it was clear that the squad ethic, which had been developed over the previous couple of years, allowed holes to be plugged, in the same way that Wales's scrambling defence in the final minutes that afternoon had filled gaps as soon as they had appeared.

'France was the crucial game for Wales,' said Hansen. 'They retained their focus in the heat of battle and showed how they had matured as a group of players. They knew they could get the job done because of the lessons they had learned along the way. When we returned from the 2003 World Cup, there were a number of times when we were in the shed after an international cursing a game that had got away from us. They needed one victory, an ugly win, to kick start it all and they got it against England. It made all the difference: when I left to go back to New Zealand, I predicted Wales would win the Six Nations within two years. I always had faith in them, but it takes time to develop a winning side. They have had another year training together and the tight five is 12 months older; and their best is still to come.'

It was, said Martyn Williams as he returned to Cardiff-Wales Airport where, for the first time since they had returned from the last World Cup, a legion of supporters was waiting to greet them, the most surreal five minutes he had experienced on a rugby pitch at the start of the second half. 'When Alfie [Gareth Thomas] was unable to come out for the second period because he had broken his thumb, it gave us an added spur,' said Williams. 'We wanted to do it for him. He has been so important to the squad: he inspires us all and sets the lead for us to follow.' The immediate feeling of the players when the whistle went was one of relief because they had been desperate for the referee to hurry up and blow for time. France were to show a fortnight later in Dublin that they were arguably the most complete team in the championship, a side for all seasons, able to play it tight or wide, but they had a larger turning circle than Wales, and when Stephen Jones started running the ball and the game they found themselves not waving but drowning.

CHAPTER 6

Guitar Man

Winning can be defined as the science of
being totally prepared.

George Allen

ANYONE VISITING THE WALES SQUAD'S VALE OF GLAMORGAN
hotel in the early hours of the Sunday morning after Wales had
secured their first Grand Slam for 27 years having beaten Ireland,
and expecting riotous celebrations, would have been taken aback
to have seen the Wales coach Mike Ruddock sitting in the foyer,
strumming his guitar and singing songs. Ruddock plays in a band
called Mid Life Crisis, but crisis, a word used so often about
Welsh rugby in the previous two decades, did not strike any kind
of a chord. 'I missed Mike's effort because I was celebrating
elsewhere, but by all accounts it was superb,' said Mark Taylor,
who had been called into the side to face Ireland just 24 hours
before the kick-off after Rhys Williams and Hal Luscombe were
ruled out with injuries. Taylor played on the wing rather than in

his accustomed position in the centre. 'I joined Swansea in 1995 when Mike was the coach; he would always pull his guitar out when we had a function at the end of a season. Some of the players were in the foyer singing along with Mike, while others of us were in Cardiff city centre, soaking up the atmosphere and not wanting one of the best days of our lives to end.'

It was a day Ruddock had long aspired to. He had started his coaching career with Blaina, the Gwent village where he had been born and where he had commenced his career as a wing forward. In 1978, Wales's last Grand Slam year, he had been part of the Blaina Youth side which had won the Welsh Youth Cup, a notable achievement for what was considered a junior club. Tredegar was his first stop in first-class rugby and he then moved on to Swansea where he made 119 appearances and scored 43 tries. His playing career was ended prematurely at the age of 27 when, working as an electricity linesman, he was knocked off a telegraph pole by a passing lorry and fell 30 feet to the ground. He suffered a fractured skull, three compressed vertebrae and impaired hearing in one ear. After leaving hospital, where he had spent two months, he tried to regain his fitness by running along the roads around Blaina, but the hard surfaces jarred his back and he asked to join Blaina's training sessions so he could jog on grass. Within weeks, he had been asked to take charge of the forwards and the following season found himself coaching the side.

'I never set out to be a coach,' said Ruddock. 'It happened by chance and I quickly discovered that it was something I enjoyed.' He led Blaina to a district championship before moving to Cross Keys, another Gwent club, but one which had first-class status. Keys had fallen on hard times after celebrating their centenary in 1985–86, losing 37 of their 47 matches the following season. In 1989–90 under Ruddock, they recorded 25 victories in 45 starts, the first time they had actually ended a campaign in credit since

1975–76. They finished that season in 12th position in the unofficial *Western Mail* club championship, their highest placing for 25 years – national leagues were to start the following season. Their victims included Swansea, defeated 16–13 at Keys' picturesque Pandy Park ground, and while Ruddock went on to enjoy coaching success with Swansea, Leinster and Wales, his achievement at Cross Keys, where the only resources he had to work with were his own, showed him to be a coach of rare quality.

'When Mike agreed to coach the club, he said from the start that if he had a call from Swansea he would go straight away,' recalled the Cross Keys club historian, Horace Jefferies. 'He said Swansea was where his heart was and that he believed he would one day have the chance to do the job he craved. Mike was always up front and honest, someone you could talk to. Some coaches are prickly when committee men or supporters challenge them on tactics or selection, but Mike would always take the trouble to sit you down and explain exactly why he had taken a certain course of action. He spent two seasons with us and he made a huge difference: under Mike, the club regained its self-respect. We always knew he would go on to bigger and better things and I am not at all surprised that he made an immediate impact with Wales.'

Ruddock's first match in charge of Cross Keys was on a West Country tour. They had arranged two matches in Devon and they found themselves in Brixham for their opening game. 'Mike felt he needed to take the players away so that he could get to know them,' said Jefferies. 'I remember him remarking that they would go there as strangers and return bound by a camaraderie which would serve them through the season, and he was right. The game against Brixham was going well until the end: we were leading by a point, but the referee had played a huge amount of stoppage time until they were awarded a penalty, which they kicked to win the game. Mike had a word with the English referee afterwards and we did not hang around in the clubhouse, having been treated terribly. As we waited to board the coach outside the club to go back to our hotel, the driver reversed over Mike's cherished guitar. Mike looked at me, then at the driver and it is fair to say that he was not best pleased. He loved his music and often brought his guitar into the clubhouse in order to, in his word, jam.'

The first thing Ruddock did at Cross Keys was stiffen their pack. 'He brought in a tight-head prop from Machen, Dai Crane,' said Jefferies. 'Dai was as hard as nails and Mike soon had eight forwards who did the job he asked of them. We did not have any stars, but when they stuffed the ball up their jumpers, it took some getting off them. Mike used to say that there were three stages to building a side: get the forwards right, mould a set of backs capable of playing expansive rugby and then get everyone into a state of mind which would allow them to react to events on the field as they saw them, able to change the course of a game tactically on their own initiative. The last part was easier said than done at a club like Keys, which did not attract elite players. I remember one game where one of our second rows, Martyn Williams [not to be confused with the flanker of the same name who was an integral part of Ruddock's Grand Slam-winning side], was having trouble with his opposite number in the lineout. Martyn was called Spanner because he worked as a fitter and this guy was getting in front of him in the lineouts and nicking the ball. Mike was standing on the sideline and shouted out: "Spanner, use your head." No sooner had Mike said it than Spanner nutted the bloke and, as all hell broke loose, Mike covered his face with his hands. I suspect he does not have the same communication problems today.'

If it was at Cross Keys where Ruddock showed his potential as a coach, it was at Swansea where he fulfilled it. Pre-Ruddock, Swansea were consistent only in their inconsistency. They had finished the first league season third from the bottom of the Premier Division and had lost to the team immediately below them, Glamorgan Wanderers. In the December, they had defeated Pontypool 63–6 in the league at St Helen's, only to lose to the same opponents 28–10 in the semi-final of the Welsh Cup less than five months later. Their coach, Alun Donovan, a former Wales centre who had had a distinguished career with Swansea and Cardiff, resigned at the end of the campaign. Ruddock, who was then ending his first year in charge of the Dublin club Bective Rangers, was driving in the Irish capital trying to listen, in between the crackles, to Radio Wales and managed to hear that Swansea were looking for a new coach. He made immediate contact with the club's then chairman, Mike James, and he was chosen ahead of other, more fancied candidates. When Ruddock was appointed as the Wales coach in the summer of 2004, the man he brought in as his advisor was Donovan, an imaginative thinker about the game whose talents had, for the past decade, been scandalously under-utilised. Every time a television camera panned to Ruddock in the Wales management's box at the Millennium Stadium in their two home matches in the Grand Slam year, Donovan could be seen sitting on the coach's immediate left, looking, in his 50th year, pretty much as he had done in his playing days.

Ruddock's first signing when he joined Swansea was the Pontypool hooker Garin Jenkins, who was to go on to win 58 Wales caps. Ruddock's priority, as it had been at Cross Keys, was to fortify a pack which had been regarded as a soft touch. 'We have to be able to graft when required,' Ruddock had said at the start of that campaign. 'We need to show more discipline up front and our aim is to finish in the top four.' Ruddock was to say before Wales's final match of the 2005 Six Nations that, if he had made a difference since taking over from Steve Hansen the previous year, it was finding the extra 1 per cent needed to turn potential into achievement. 'I have always believed in the importance of planning,' he said, referring to his early years as Swansea's coach when setting a trend in a sport which was then still played and administered by amateurs. Knowing from his days as a player that Swansea's form was as variable as the weather, he immediately set about changing the mindset of the players. Garin Jenkins hardly fitted the image of an archetypal Swansea player: a student of the game's darker arts, he got himself into the record books at the end of the 1980s when the Welsh Rugby Union introduced the sin-bin to allow hot-headed players ten minutes of reflection; playing for Pontypridd at Newbridge, Jenkins found himself heading for the cooler straight from the kick-off.

'Mike appreciated that rugby, no matter what style of play you prefer, starts with the basics,' said Jenkins, who retired from international rugby in 2000 after ten years at the top. 'One of the differences between Mike's Wales side and that of his predecessor Steve Hansen is that our set-pieces have improved considerably. I do not think it is a coincidence that we have started to win matches we were losing narrowly before. Mike placed great store on the mental side of the game, and he was always receptive to ideas: when we went to the Gnoll to face Neath in the sixth round of the Welsh Cup in 1995, we had only won at the ground once in some 14 years. At a team meeting a couple of days before the match, I had suggested that we only take our change strip with us: it was a dark blue and I knew that our wearing the strip would force Neath to use their change kit instead of their traditional black. My thought was that if anyone in the Swansea team had a hang-up about Neath, their black jersey would symbolise it: Neath loved being the bad guys in black. Mike embraced the idea and as soon as we got to the ground and Neath found out what we were up to, they went mad: one of their officials had our kit man by the throat, telling him to get hold of some of our traditional white jerseys. Neath ended up wearing some horrible turquoise strip: we had won the mind games and we went on to win the match [22–20].'

Earlier that season Swansea had defeated Australia – the country which a year before had routed Wales 63–6 in Brisbane and 38–3 in Cardiff in the World Cup – on a rousing afternoon at St Helen's. Tries by Garin Jenkins and the centre Scott Gibbs, another player enticed by Ruddock to Swansea during the coach's first season at the club, took the All Whites to a 21–6 victory which, for many years, Ruddock rated as his best moment in the game. 'The key to that victory was the dominance we established up front,' said Jenkins. 'Mike had started the build-up for the game the previous summer when we went on tour to Canada: we were out there for two weeks, and although we had a bit of fun, the training sessions were hard work. We started the league campaign with a bang, winning our first 12 matches, and we were at the top of our game by the time we faced the Wallabies. Mike was always meticulous in his preparations: he never left anything to chance.'

One of Ruddock's first acts after taking charge at Swansea was to bring in a sports scientist, Andy Smith, to help in the side's mental preparations. 'Swansea have always been able to produce one-off performances,' said Ruddock at the time, 'but to win the league, you have to be the most consistent team over a gruelling 18-match programme.' Swansea not only went on to become champions, but also reached the final of the Welsh Cup, losing to their arch-rivals, Llanelli, 16–7. 'We ended up showing more discipline up front, we learned how to really graft when we needed to and we displayed greater maturity,' said Ruddock. 'Our aim now has to be to perform at high levels every season.' Swansea finished third in the league the following season and went back to the top in 1994–95, when they won 20 matches out of 22, becoming the first club to claim the title for a second time.

In his foreword to Garin Jenkins's autobiography, *In the Eye of the Storm*, published in 2000, Ruddock outlined his approach when he arrived at Swansea. 'After my first training session with the squad, I initiated a brainstorming session entitled "The Way Forward",' Ruddock wrote. 'I asked the players to analyse the contemporary rugby environment and consider three recommendations for improvement, which were:

1 The need for a clearly defined management structure
2 The need for a reliable goal-kicker
3 The need for more 'dog' in the team.

'The first two recommendations could be fairly easily organised. Number three seemed more of a problem. Looking at the squad, I felt we would improve if we recruited a tough hooker. Having lived and coached in Ireland for a year, I asked around to establish the identity of the hooker in Wales that front row forwards least wanted to play against. The answer was consistent: Garin Jenkins, a hooker who would be perfect for the gameplan I wanted to adopt. The boys from Pontypool always liked to scrummage hard, and I wanted to build a pack of enforcers who would turn Swansea into a fearsome scrummaging outfit. I knew of Swansea's tradition of running rugby and wanted that to continue, but at the same time I wanted a better platform. I retained vivid memories of being on the wrong end of a number of hidings at Pontypool Park as a result of Swansea's inability to hold Pooler's scrum power. I wanted the All Whites to emulate that forward power and then blend it with the depth, width and pace of the Swansea backs. Garin would be the key to that plan, and he brought a new toughness and honesty to the team.'

In his foreword, Ruddock also revealed his psychology in the build-up to the 1992 meeting with the Australians. 'In the press release which announced our team for the game, I put an asterisk alongside the names of our 12 internationals. The two exceptions at forward were the two props, the veteran Keith Colclough and the rookie Chris Clark. The only non-international behind was the wing Simon Davies, who had played for Wales A. We had a short bus journey to the ground following our pre-match team meeting, and during it I told the front row that the Wallabies had looked at the team-sheet and noticed that our two props had not achieved any honours. Our opponents therefore believed that our front row would be a weakness and they would attack us there. Of course, it was all a load of nonsense, but I walked away leaving Cloughie going ballistic. Garin started geeing up young Chris Clark, assuring him that everything would be okay. By the time the first scrum was called, the lads were really fired up. Cloughie started growling while Garin proceeded to explain to his world-renowned opposite number, Phil Kearns [the Wallaby captain], that Mr Garin Jenkins was in fact the world's number one hooker, and not Mr Kearns. The dip and drive came on and we blasted the Aussie pack to pieces. Their scrum went backwards the whole game.'

Swansea won the Welsh Cup under Ruddock in 1995, defeating Pontypridd 17–12 in the final, the first time they had lifted the trophy since 1978. They had defeated Cardiff 16–9 in a hard-fought semi-final that had gone to extra time, a match which had seen Ruddock get one over on his opposite number, Alex Evans, a few weeks after the pair, along with the Pontypridd coach Dennis John, had been put in charge of Wales's World Cup campaign that summer following the resignation of Alan Davies and his national management team. Evans headed up the triumvirate, with John coaching the backs and Ruddock responsible for the forwards. They only had six weeks to prepare triumvirate, with John coaching the backs and Ruddock responsible for the forwards. They only had six weeks to prepare for the World Cup and Wales, who had been whitewashed in the 1995 Five Nations, failed to make the quarter-finals after losing to New Zealand and then Ireland in Johannesburg. Evans had prevailed in selection with seven Cardiff players included in the final group match against the Irish, by which time the squad had divided on tribal lines.

When he returned to Wales, Evans gave an interview to a rugby magazine, *First XV*, in which he suggested that Ruddock had cooperated with players who were slipping out of their hotel at night for a drink during the World Cup. Evans was quoted as saying that the armed security guards, who had been detailed to accompany members of the squad every time they left the hotel, had complained to him that they were fed up with being kept out until four or five in the morning. The remarks caused a furore, with Swansea and Ruddock, in particular, incensed. Evans, while not apologising, said that he had made the comments off the record and regretted that they had been published. However, he stood by his contention that, while Wales had sufficient talent to regain their place at world rugby's top table, they would continue to dine off crumbs until players realised the sacrifices they had to make if they were going to succeed.

'Alex was a very good coach with a number of new ideas,' said Garin Jenkins, 'but he did not understand the Welsh psyche. We spent our first two weeks in South Africa banged up in a hotel in Bloemfontein and saw nothing but its walls. What Mike appreciated, in a way that Alex did not, was that there were times when the players had to be allowed to relax. The stories about players falling out and going out boozing were blown up out of all proportion. Alex had stuffed the squad with Cardiff players and given the captaincy to his club skipper, Mike Hall, but you could which was make-or-break because the losers would be flying home, Alex said that passion did not win matches. We were beaten inside 20 minutes as Ireland tore into us with a passion-drenched fury: we were as cold as ice.

'Mike is one of the best coaches produced by Wales and one of his strengths is that he knows when it is time for players to chill out: after Wales had beaten France in the 2005 Six Nations, some of the management wanted the boys to have a quiet night in. Mike would have none of it and told the players to go out and have a few beers. He trusted the players not to take advantage, and he clearly pressed the right buttons because they started the next game in Scotland on fire. He wants the team to play with smiles on their faces, and that cannot happen unless they are allowed to let their hair down occasionally. It is all about understanding our culture and Graham Henry was getting there at the end of his time with Wales. He had started to give players more of a role in decision-making and he was the one who first appreciated that we were not taking advantage of the fact that we were a small country: it was easy to gather the national squad together on a regular basis and form what was effectively a club side, something none of the other major countries could do.'

Alex Evans took Wales to South Africa for a one-off international in September 1995, their first in the professional era, but he said he did not want the job on a full-time basis and the former London Welsh coach Kevin Bowring was appointed. Before the World Cup, Ruddock had been regarded as the favourite to succeed Alan Davies but, after the WRU had named him one of Evans's assistants at the 1995 World Cup, a leaflet which questioned Ruddock's credentials was passed around at a meeting of the Union's general committee. It cited Swansea's 78–7 defeat to South Africa at St Helen's the previous autumn, their mid-table position in the league and a shock home defeat to a struggling Abertillery side; his achievements were not listed, and the bizarre episode showed the deep divisions within the Welsh game at the time. Ruddock remained at Swansea until the end of the 1996–97 season, but they did not win any more trophies under him. His final match in charge was the 1997 Welsh Cup final against Cardiff, who won a pulsating contest 33–26. Ruddock's title then was director of coaching, reflecting the way rugby had changed in the two years of professionalism, with coaches responsible for considerably more than preparing their teams on the training field. Ruddock, though, had almost been a professional in the amateur era. 'I was fortunate that when I started at Swansea, I worked for a company which had links to the rugby club,' said Ruddock. 'I was given time during the day to devote to coaching. I even had my own room at St Helen's, almost unheard of then, which allowed me to look at videos of other teams in action and prepare for matches accordingly.'

Ruddock analysed opponents in detail, adjusting his tactics accordingly, and he also took account of who the referee for Swansea's next match was, noting which offences the official had a low tolerance threshold for and what he tended to allow players to get away with. 'Mike had a winning mentality,' said Garin Jenkins. 'He made Swansea a force again, but what he also did was to establish a development programme at the club which not only benefited the club but Wales as well. He got me working as a schools' development officer, broadening my horizons, and helping me develop coaching skills he believed would stand me in good stead in the years to come.'

As the coaching director of Leinster, where he spent three years from 1997, Ruddock guided them to an inter-provincial championship. The Irish Rugby Football Union was then more cosmopolitan in its outlook than the other home unions: the national side was coached by an Englishman, the innovative Brian

JUST KICK IT: Gavin Henson sets Wales on their way to Grand Slam glory with a 50-metre penalty to sink England. (© Getty Images)

JUST WILLIAMS: Wales wing Shane Williams crosses for the only try of the game against England. (© Getty Images)

GETTING A LIFT: Gavin Henson gives 18-year-old England centre Mathew Tait a rude introduction to international rugby. (© Getty Images)

DONE IT: Wales second row Robert Sidoli celebrates his first taste of victory over England. (© Getty Images)

EXCUSE ME: Second row Brent Cockbain bursts away for his first try in international rugby during Wales's victory over Italy in Rome.
(© Getty Images)

EVEN IN THE QUIETEST MOMENTS: Wales coach Mike Ruddock is caught in contemplative mood in Rome.
(© Getty Images)

LEADING FROM THE FRONT: Wales's front row was writte[n] off before the Six Nations, but Adam Jones, Mefin Davie[s] and Gethin Jenkins had the last laugh. (© Getty Images)

PEELING OFF: Scrum-half Dwayne Peel, a key figure in Wales's high-tempo game, lifts the pace against France in Paris. (© Getty Images)

OVER AND OUT: Outside-half Stephen Jones, the man of the match in Paris, celebrates his crucial late drop goal with Gavin Henson. (© Getty Images)

NO PAIN, NO GAIN: Wales captain Gareth Thomas celebrates the victory over France – you would never guess he had broken his right thumb in five places. (© Getty Images)

FLY NOW: Wing Rhys Williams sets off on his 75-metre dash to the Scotland try-line to put Wales 14–0 up at Murrayfield. (© Getty Images)

CREAM OF THE CROP:
Wales flanker Martyn
Williams, later voted man
of the Six Nations, says
au revoir to the French.
(© Getty Images)

JUST FOR KICKS: The
silver-booted Gavin
Henson proves a golden
shot again with a 55-
metre penalty against
Ireland.
(© Getty Images)

CUP OF CHEER: Former Pontypridd colleagues Mar
Williams and Kevin Morgan clutch the Six Nations trop
(© Getty Imag

Ashton, who was succeeded by two New Zealanders, Murray Kidd and Warren Gatland. During his time with Leinster, Ruddock was one of the first to appreciate the potential of Brian O'Driscoll and gave the centre his first professional break. O'Driscoll quickly went on to establish himself as the leading outside-centre in the world; when Ruddock was appointed as the Wales coach in 2004, O'Driscoll paid him a fulsome tribute, saying presciently that, based on his experiences at Leinster under the Welshman, he did not expect it to be long before Wales were challenging again at the top. Ruddock regarded his greatest achievement at Leinster as their 32–10 Heineken Cup victory at Leicester in the 1999–2000 season (under Ruddock, Swansea had made the semi-final of the inaugural Heineken Cup in 1996, when they lost away to Toulouse); no other team was to win at the Tigers' Welford Road lair for more than three years. When Ruddock left for Ireland, the Llanelli coach Gareth Jenkins, the man Ruddock was to pip for the Wales coaching job, described the move as a 'disaster' for Welsh rugby and questioned why the WRU had not done everything in its power to keep him in the country. 'He understands the game in Wales and his departure sends out the wrong message at a vital time,' said Jenkins. 'Someone of his calibre should have a role to play in the national scheme of things.' Ruddock said his decision to return to Ireland – his wife, Bernadette, is Irish – was made because he had ambitions to coach Wales: broadening his horizons would, he felt, give him a more impressive cv, and his experience in Ireland counted in his favour when he and Jenkins, who had spent all his rugby career in Wales, vied to succeed Hansen. 'My aim is to coach a national side and this move will allow me to prove myself at a higher level,' he said. 'I do not rule out a return to Wales. The game is now professional and coaches have to grasp opportunities as well as players. Welsh rugby needs a structure to move it forward whereas the set-up in Ireland is good: their four provinces each have 25 players contracted to the Irish Rugby Football Union with proper back-up facilities.'

Ireland proved more receptive to Ruddock's vision than his homeland. Before he left for Leinster, Ruddock proposed that Wales should try to get four of its clubs into the English league to improve the quality of competition and ensure that the best players were concentrated in those sides. It did not happen – the WRU rejected an eventual proposal by the Rugby Football Union to include three Welsh clubs in the top division in England with two more in the division below – but Ruddock's contention that the Welsh game could not sustain eight or nine professional clubs was subsequently borne out by events; he is today working, as he envisaged seven years ago, in a system underpinned by four elite professional teams. He gained representative experience in Ireland coaching the national A team and was called into some senior squad sessions by Ashton to help with organising the lineout. By 2000, he had reached the point where he realised that if he were to remain in Ireland, his chances of coaching Wales would recede with each passing year; and, anyway, Henry, who had replaced Bowring in the summer of 1998, wanted Ruddock back in the Principality.

'We were very sorry to see Mike go,' said Ken Ging, Leinster's team manager during Ruddock's time in Ireland. 'He was our first professional coach and he fast-tracked a number of young players such as Brian O'Driscoll and Shane Horgan. He always encouraged players to express themselves and he always mixed things up in training: he would hold an all-Ireland hurling or Gaelic football final the one day and organise a cricket match the next. He had a sense of fun, but he would tear strips off players if they stepped out of line. He is an all-round nice guy. When I had heart surgery, Mike spent all night at the hospital with my wife until they knew the operation had been successful. He has always kept in touch since leaving Ireland, and has proved very adept at text messaging.'

Ruddock returned to Wales at the start of the 2000–01 season and became Ebbw Vale's head coach. Part of the inducement behind his return was the promise that he would become the Wales A coach, but no sooner had Ruddock settled in at Vale, starting, as he had at Swansea, by announcing his bold playing plans for the future, than the club was rocked by financial problems; a number of players left and the former Wales internationals Byron Hayward and Kingsley Jones were included in a cull of the highest earners. Forced to revise his ambition of moulding Vale into a title contender, he turned them into a team capable of rising to the one-off occasion and they twice made the semi-finals of the Welsh Cup. When, in 2003, Wales moved from a club to a regional system, Ruddock was not regarded as the favourite to become the head coach of the Gwent Dragons, a team run by Ebbw Vale and Newport; even when he was appointed, the Dragons were regarded as the runt of the regional litter and the weakest of the five new sides because most of the players they ended up recruiting had not been wanted by the other teams, leading one observer to describe the Dragons as cast-offs. The Pontypridd number 8 Michael Owen, who turned down the opportunity to sign for Celtic Warriors, the region his club served, was sold by Ruddock's vision and became the Dragons' major signing. Waifs and strays they may have been written off as, but the Dragons remained in contention for the Celtic League title until the final day of the season; unlike their rivals, they had not been badly affected by the 2003 World Cup, which saw the other four regions forced to field depleted sides for the first two months of the campaign because a number of their players were with Wales in Australia.

'We did not play the rugby under Mike that Wales were to in the 2005 Six Nations, but that was because we did not have the players to do so,' said Owen. 'What he did was organise us and make us competitive at forward. We were a team that was hard to beat and Mike made sure that the players were a tight unit: there were no stars. We surprised a lot of people, but not ourselves. I joined the Dragons because I knew Mike could improve me as a player: everyone I spoke to had the highest regard for him and it was a decision that I never came to regret.'

Shortly after Wales returned from the 2003 World Cup, Steve Hansen confirmed his intention to return to New Zealand at the end of the following year's Six Nations campaign. The WRU advertised for his job and Ruddock was widely expected to apply. In January 2004, he announced that he would not be answering the advertisement because he did not feel that the time was right for him. He said he wanted to spend at least two more years with the Dragons to complete what he had started and recommended that Gareth Jenkins, the head coach of Llanelli Scarlets, who had been part of Alan Davies's Wales management team between 1992 and 1995, take over from Hansen. Jenkins, a passionate, innovative coach who had enjoyed considerable success at Llanelli having, like Ruddock, turned to coaching early after his playing career had been prematurely ended by injury, was regarded as the people's favourite, and Ruddock, who had not forgotten how the prize had been snatched from his hands in 1998, when the WRU turned to Graham Henry having all but offered Ruddock the job, had also applied for the job of forwards coach at the end of 2001, losing out to Hansen. He was not ready to risk another rejection.

The WRU set up a five-man panel to interview the applicants and recommend Hansen's successor. It was made up of four WRU officials: the chief executive David Moffett, the general manager

GUITAR MAN

Steve Lewis, the chairman David Pickering and the director of rugby Terry Cobner, together with David Rees, a member of the Union's board, previously known as the general committee. Two short-listed candidates were invited back for a second interview: Jenkins and Mark Evans, the chief executive and head coach of the London club Harlequins, a 44 year old who had been born in England but raised in Cardiff. The Welsh media were leaked information that Evans had done well at interview and that the appointment of Jenkins was anything but a foregone conclusion. In hindsight, it appears it was a concerted attempt to prepare the Welsh rugby public for someone other than Jenkins to take over from Hansen. Before Moffett's arrival in December 2002, the WRU had leaked information profusely, but he quickly succeeded in reducing the flow of information. The complete fooling of the media when the new Wales coach was unveiled, with no one expecting Ruddock to walk through the door, raised suspicions that he had been the Union's preferred candidate for some while.

Which is not to suggest that the five-man panel did not have open minds. When Jenkins gave his first interview, he stressed the importance of a four-year development programme. His vision of the future encompassed far more than the national side, but the Union, up to its neck in debt and struggling to finance the regional system adequately, did not want to hear the word development. Jenkins and Evans were asked what they would have done had they won the toss before Wales's international against Ireland at Lansdowne Road the previous February: would they have instructed their captain to take first use of the wind or give it to the opposition? The question gave a clue to the way the panel was thinking: it wanted a coach who would wrap himself up in the Wales squad and leave the politics to others, perhaps not surprising after six years of interfering New Zealanders who had kicked down closed doors; there was also an acceptance, perhaps, that Hansen was leaving behind him a firm construction which did not need to be demolished and rebuilt. Jenkins, like his mentor at Llanelli in the 1970s, Carwyn James, was doomed to miss out on the job he so coveted.

As Jenkins and Evans had been invited back for their second interviews in March 2004, Ruddock was asked whether he could consider making himself available for the job. 'I had come to regret my decision not to apply originally,' he said later. 'I reflected that I deserved the opportunity after working for 20 years at the coalface.' Ruddock, unbeknown to the other two candidates, was interviewed and invited to take up the post after making a two-hour presentation to the panel. It was an offer which he accepted with alacrity. A media conference scheduled to announce Hansen's successor was not deemed particularly newsworthy outside Wales, though when its start was delayed by an hour, ostensibly because the WRU's board was taking more time than expected to confirm the panel's recommendation, some thought that Evans had got the nod over Jenkins. Even when Ruddock walked into the room where the announcement was to be made, very few of those present realised what was going on.

Ruddock's reign did not get off to a quiet start. Reaction to his appointment in Wales west of Swansea was one of angry indignation after it was revealed that the WRU had gone ahead with the media conference despite not being able to get hold of Jenkins, who had told Union officials that he would be at a funeral in the early afternoon. Jenkins learned that someone who had not applied for the job had been appointed after one of his Llanelli Scarlets' players, the prop John Davies, rang to ask what he thought of the news. The Union's satisfaction at catching the media with their pants down was replaced by days of fire-fighting with Jenkins saying he had been publicly humiliated. Whether the right or wrong appointment had been made was a matter of opinion; a poll in the *Western Mail* backed Ruddock by an overwhelming margin. It was the manner in which the WRU had gone about things which rankled. Jenkins made it clear that by denouncing the Union, he was not implying that it had made a poor choice in Ruddock; he merely felt like a player who, lulled into believing that a cherished first cap would be his, had failed to hear his name when the team was read out.

'I know what Gareth is going through because I have been there myself in 1998 and my heart goes out to him,' said Ruddock, after securing the job. 'My appointment was the Union's call and they obviously felt that something was missing. I have a huge respect for Gareth and I will be contacting him in the next week or so. He, and all the other regional coaches, has a huge part to play in the future.' Ruddock kept to his word and went to Llanelli to meet Jenkins. At the beginning of the week when Wales played England in the 2005 Six Nations, the Welsh squad was given a two-hour presentation on the strength and weaknesses of the World Cup holders. It was made by Jenkins, who had been asked by Ruddock to follow England in the November series of internationals; if the move said everything about Ruddock, who recognised that the only way to reduce the friction, which had always seemed to exist between club/region and country, to a minimum was to involve the regions in the national set-up, it also spoke volumes for Jenkins, who set aside his personal disappointment in what must have been a bittersweet moment for him.

In his first taste of coaching at international level in the 1995 World Cup, Ruddock had experienced the damage wreaked by internal division. As a consequence of that unhappy memory, at the start of the 2004–05 season he asked all four regions to make presentations to the squad on different teams in the Six Nations Championship: Gareth Jenkins was given England; the Dragons' coach Leigh Jones monitored France; the Neath-Swansea Ospreys' coach Sean Holley watched Scotland; and the Cardiff Blues' backs coach Geraint John scrutinised Ireland. Italy was left to Alun Donovan, Ruddock's predecessor as the Swansea coach in the early 1990s. The pair had been Swansea teammates the previous decade. Donovan had been out of the game since leaving Cardiff's coaching team in the mid-1990s. Ruddock had asked him at the end of 2003 to do some scouting work for the Dragons, watching all the Gwent clubs in the Welsh Premier Division – Newport, Pontypool, Ebbw Vale, Newbridge, Cross Keys and Bedwas – with a view to identifying potential regional players of the future.

'Mike had a vision of making the Dragons an all-Gwent team,' said Donovan. 'I had known him for more than 25 years and we regularly talked together. I had been out of rugby for a while and was happy to do a little bit again. Mike has never been someone who thought he knew all the answers and he likes the exchange of ideas. He is a loyal guy: we had worked together closely before and I had no hesitation in taking him up on his offer. Everybody had predicted that the Dragons would fail, but if you look at the story of Mike's coaching career, from the days he started out at Blaina, he always makes the most of what he has at his disposal. He never makes excuses, he just gets on with things.'

Ruddock's second job as the Wales coach was to take the squad on a three-Test tour to the southern hemisphere: the side had two international matches in Argentina followed by a one-off Test in South Africa, a ludicrous enough itinerary at any time, but considering Wales had been involved in the World Cup in Australia eight months before, it made even less sense. His first task had been Wales's friendly clash against the Barbarians at Bristol City's Ashton Gate on 26 May. The Baa-Baas were routed 42–0. 'I could feel a difference with Wales that day,' said the

France international Thomas Castaignede, who had come on as a half-time replacement. 'We turned up with a slightly lackadaisical attitude, but we might have got away with it against Wales teams of the past. I tipped Wales to finish fourth in the 2005 Six Nations, basing my reasoning on the fact that Wales had not beaten a major rugby nation for several years and, even if there were suggestions that they could manage it, there was no reason to believe they could string together several big games. In that sense, they were a revelation.'

The summer tour was less successful. Ruddock had to do without 14 players, including Gareth Thomas, Stephen Jones, Robin McBryde, Martyn Williams and Gareth Cooper, who were either injured or in desperate need of a rest. Wales lost the first Test against Argentina, 50–44 in Tucuman, rallying after trailing by 38–8 at the start of the second half, but they proved too strong in Buenos Aires the following week with Shane Williams running in a hat-trick of tries in the 35–20 triumph. A week later Wales were in Pretoria, playing South Africa at altitude. Injuries had further reduced Ruddock's options: Gavin Henson, who had started at inside-centre in Tucuman, played at full-back in the final two Tests, and he was exposed by the Springboks, who took advantage of an absurdly arduous tour to win 53–18.

On his return to Wales, Ruddock started preparing in earnest for the November internationals against South Africa and New Zealand, and the Six Nations. He asked Donovan to become his selection advisor, an unpaid role which would involve sitting in on selection meetings, though not having a vote, and being involved in the build-up to games. 'I had no hesitation in saying yes,' said Donovan. 'Mike and I have always seen eye-to-eye on how we feel rugby should be played, using width and pace, but making sure the platform is laid up front. My one concern was whether the other members of the team management would accept me, particularly when I sat in on their meetings, but they put me at ease from the first minute. Like Mike, Scott Johnson is receptive to ideas and relishes chewing things over.

'Mike asks the right questions of people and is honest with everyone. As a player, he was one of the hardest back row forwards of his generation. I am sure that if he had not been injured at the midway point of his senior career he would have been capped. He had played for Wales B and I always felt it was just a matter of time before he made the step up. We will never know, but his experience means that Mike will not give away caps cheaply as a coach. To him, they have to be earned, and that is how it should be. He likes to take his time making decisions and he appreciates the opinions of others: he would like to expand the management team and bring in more specialist coaches, but finances will determine that.'

As a former international inside-centre, Donovan has played close attention to the development of Henson. 'Wales needed an inside-centre to replace Iestyn Harris, and from early on in the season, Gavin fitted the bill, even though he was playing at outside-half for the Ospreys,' said Donovan. 'He was a big bloke, a powerful tackler, he had a huge kick, he could break and he could pass the ball. He was the perfect foil for Stephen Jones at outside-half and the pair have worked well together. The thing about Gavin for me is that the best is still to come from him: he has dumped players like Brian O'Driscoll, Julian White and Gordon Bulloch on their backsides and he has kicked some huge penalties, but we will see more from him in the areas of breaking the line with the ball in hand and line-kicking. He is still a young man learning his way and there was never any danger that Mike would not go for a footballing inside-centre. When people see me on television at the Millennium Stadium talking to Mike, they think that I am the one urging more width in our game, but he is

GUITAR MAN

the one who gets excited, shouting run it, while I am more cautious. The exciting rugby that Wales have played under Mike has not come about by accident, as it may have done when Wales played New Zealand in the 2003 World Cup and set the tournament alight; what we have seen since November 2004 has been the style of rugby Mike prefers. He deserves every credit for encouraging the players to express themselves fully and, when you consider how the likes of Stephen Jones, Tom Shanklin, Brent Cockbain, Ryan Jones and others have come on in the last year, it is a tribute to the management team.

'One of the differences Mike has made is that he has involved the regions in the national set-up. They agreed to release their international squad players at various times during the season, and there was goodwill where too often in the past there had been acrimony. One of Mike's strengths is his ability to get everyone working together: he does not pretend to know it all. His forte is the lineout, and that area improved immediately under him, while he brought in Stuart Evans [the Swansea, Neath and Wales prop in the 1980s] to help out with scrummaging, another area which probably cost Wales in the 2004 Six Nations. Mike works incredibly hard, he pays total attention to detail and he is always looking for the extra 1 per cent, as he calls it, which separates winners from losers, but he makes sure that the players never feel what they are doing is a drudge. Mike knows when to relax and he has not forgotten what drove him as a player.'

The sight of Ruddock relaxing with a guitar in his hands has been a common theme from Blaina through to the Wales squad's hotel. 'My career at Swansea under Mike survived an appalling incident,' said Garin Jenkins. 'We had just played British Columbia and beaten them, even though they had fielded 13 internationals. We were having a few drinks in the bar afterwards and Mike's guitar, which went everywhere with him, was lying around. Someone decided to do a Pete Townshend impression and started smashing the thing up. It might have been me: all I am saying is that the culprit lived to tell the tale.'

CHAPTER 7

Flaming Red

It's all up to what you value,
Down to where you are.
It all swings on the pain you've gone through,
Getting where you are.

George Harrison

WALES'S NEXT ENCOUNTER AFTER FRANCE WAS SCOTLAND –
from the sublime to the ridiculed – but as encounters went it was
not remotely close. There was a 15-day gap between the matches,
but it was not long enough for Gareth Thomas to recover from the
multiple fractures of his right thumb, broken in five places
towards the end of the first half at the Stade de France. The
prospect of facing the Scots at Murrayfield would not ordinarily
have daunted any side with a vestige of self-belief: Scotland
resembled the Wales of the early 1990s, shapeless, soulless and
scarred by the civil war which was being waged off the field. Even
when Welsh rugby was going through its darkest moments, and

there were a few of those, set-backs were greeted by outrage, indignation, incredulity and disgust: columns of letters in the Welsh newspapers were devoted to observations and advice, while radio phone-ins never went short of callers. Scotland's decline, in contrast, appeared to generate more in the way of apathy: the 2005 Six Nations match against Wales was not a sell-out, even though an estimated 40,000 visiting supporters swelled the attendance, outnumbering the home support by more than two to one.

Scotland may have been at their lowest ebb for many years, but Murrayfield had been a graveyard for Welsh hopes so often in the past that not even the most sanguine fan in red would have dared to predict what would happen in the opening 18 minutes. When Wales announced their side for the game in a press release, it was pointed out that Wales had travelled to Edinburgh with the championship in their sights on 15 previous occasions and had come away with a defeat every time. Legend has it that the day after Wales had lost to Scotland 35–10 in Inverleith in 1924, an afternoon when they had conceded eight tries in what was then their heaviest ever defeat, the players were taken to see the Forth Rail Bridge, which at the time was regarded an exceptional example of engineering. 'Take a good look at it, boys,' said Tom Schofield, one of the Welsh Rugby Union's International Rugby Board's representatives. 'It is the last time any of you will see it at the expense of the WRU.'

Wales's visit to Scotland in 1951 offered to optimistic home supporters a parallel to 2005. The Scots had then been given no chance against a side which had won the Grand Slam the previous year and which had started off the new Five Nations campaign with a thumping 23–5 victory over England at St Helen's. Wales contained 11 Lions who had gone on the previous summer's tour to New Zealand and Australia, while Scotland had won only six of their 18 post-war internationals (they were to lose their next 17 Tests after defeating Wales). There were 25,000 Welsh spectators in the 81,000 crowd, then a record for a rugby match in Britain, but they did not have one score to celebrate as their side crashed 19–0 in what was then one of the biggest upsets in international rugby. Complacency was blamed for what came to be known as the Murrayfield Massacre and, by constantly referring to the fact that Wales had only won at the ground once in the previous 20 years, it was a mistake the Wales management resolved not to repeat in 2005.

Scotland had been whitewashed in 2004, their Australian coach Matt Williams's first season in charge, and although they had started the 2005 Six Nations with an ill-deserved defeat in Paris, they had then been trounced at home by Ireland and had narrowly got the better of Italy in a turgid match at Murrayfield, when they had been outscored on tries and were fortunate that the goal-kicking woes which had blighted Italy's 2005 campaign had continued. Williams was coming under increasing fire, even after the victory over the Azzurri, from a number of former Scottish internationals who, accepting that Scotland's decline had its roots in a domestic game which, despite constant restructuring in the professional era had failed to yield dividends in the international arena, argued that he was not taking the side anywhere. 'I have no intention of resigning and I am in it for the long haul,' Williams had said after the 40–13 defeat against Ireland. 'If you look at Ireland five years ago, they were really struggling with the same group of players who are doing well for them now. That's where our group could be in a few years.' After the end of the championship, and further heavy reverses against Wales and England, he claimed that Scotland would soon win the Six Nations, but no one was listening.

Kevin Morgan for the injured Thomas at full-back was the only change made by Wales from the Stade de France. (Despite their winning start, they had still to field an unchanged side.) The number 8 Michael Owen, who had taken over the captaincy from Thomas in the second half of the game in Paris, was named as his country's skipper for the first time. 'Captaining your country is the highest honour you can have as a player,' said Owen. 'My job was made easier by the fact that when he was the Wales coach, Steve Hansen shared out responsibilities among players so that it was not the case any more that just one man was in charge. That is still the case under Mike Ruddock: everyone is equal and there are any number of leaders in the team. I will never forget the day, though, because it was the first time I had led out the side, and the rugby we played, especially in the first half, made it all the more memorable.'

One of the lessons of the opening three weekends of the championship was that there was no more dangerous side on the counter-attack than Wales. In Morgan, Rhys Williams and Shane Williams, they had a trio capable of turning loose kicks into tries. Scotland's only hope of making a game of it was to keep the game tight, make their line kicks count and look to exploit any Welsh nerves by making their first-up tackles tell and contesting for every scrap of possession at the breakdown. It was arguably Wales's first real test of the year: they had been the underdogs against England in Cardiff and France were the favourites against them in Paris; while Wales were expected to prevail in Rome, few had anticipated that they would canter home by 30 points. Despite Mike Ruddock's attempt to play up Scotland's prospects, the overwhelming belief on that Sunday afternoon was that the only question was how many points Wales would win by. Expectation was a factor.

Scotland had to make a strong start, but little more than two minutes were on the clock when the centre Hugo Southwell, under no real pressure, kicked the ball from his own 22 into the arms of Shane Williams, who was standing on the Welsh 10-metre line. It was the invitation Wales had been hoping and indeed waiting for. 'When you are playing away from home, you know that an early score will quieten the home crowd,' said Stephen Jones, though in the case of Murrayfield that day every Wales try was greeted with a deafening roar. 'Manchester United and Arsenal had each had a tricky FA Cup tie away from home the previous day and they had both scored goals in the early minutes of their matches which laid the foundations for victory. We were determined to do the same, although we had no idea that the game would effectively be over so early.'

Shane Williams accepted Southwell's stray kick gratefully and passed to Rhys Williams in the middle of the field. He found the wing forward Ryan Jones, who charged through the two Scotland second rows, Stuart Grimes and Scott Murray, before releasing Morgan; the full-back off-loaded to the prop Gethin Jenkins and Rhys Williams again became involved in the move which, thanks to quick feet and stunning handling and passing, reached Scotland's 22. The platform for the *coup de grâce* was supplied by Martyn Williams who, rather in the manner of a centre three-quarter, took the ball under pressure and immediately fired out an arrow of a pass which landed in the arms of Ryan Jones, who stormed over the line for a score which, in a captivating 15-second passage of play, encapsulated what Ruddock's Wales were all about: they had the patience, ruthlessness and grace of a bird of prey, knowing the precise moment when to swoop for the kill.

If Scotland had revealed their self-destructive capacities through aimless play and powder-puff tackling, worse was to follow for the modest contingent of home supporters a few minutes later. The outside-half Dan Parks had endured a wretched championship, but when he received the ball on Wales's 22 with four players unmarked outside him, there seemed no way that Scotland could not draw level at 7–7. Parks, however, seemed overwhelmed by the moment and threw out a long pass to no one in particular, which was easily intercepted by Rhys Williams who was able to indulge himself in the most casual of canters before he touched the ball down under the Scottish posts. As the Scots had averaged 13.5 points in their first three games, the match already looked beyond them at 14–0 down, but, unluckily for them, Wales had only just begun.

That opening was the prelude to what the former Wales and Lions' scrum-half Gareth Edwards was later to describe as the best half of rugby he had ever seen a Welsh side produce. When the half-time whistle blew, Wales were 38–3 in front, having already scored more points against Scotland than ever before. Gerald Davies, a playing contemporary of Edwards's, wrote in *The Times*: 'There was a silky smoothness in Wales's manner that often bewildered Scotland and left them standing in a constantly changing landscape. Wales were never where Scotland expected them to be and, if they were, there were simply too many of them. There is an individual and unpredictable arc to Wales's game, a style of play that belongs uniquely to them. They are nothing if not a daring team and in a bravura style they once more stamped their maverick identity on the championship.'

Wales had started the week not sure who their hooker would be. Mefin Davies had injured the tip of a thumb in Paris while his deputy, Robin McBryde, had picked up a knee injury in the same match. Ruddock called up the Llanelli Scarlets hooker Matthew Rees as a precaution, but both Davies and McBryde were to be passed fit. If the prospect of a Grand Slam was something every member of the squad was struggling to take in, there was no one more incredulous than the 32-year-old Davies who, nine months before after returning from his stag night in Galway, found himself out of work when the Welsh Rugby Union disbanded his regional side, Celtic Warriors.

'It was totally unexpected,' said Davies. 'We had done well in the Heineken Cup that season, winning at the eventual champions, Wasps, and we had a squad we felt was good enough to make a big impact in Europe in the next couple of years. They were exciting times and we had no warning the region was going to be closed down. I was about to get married and all of a sudden I was out of a job. What made it worse was that no one came in for me and Wales were about to go on tour to Argentina and South Africa: it presented me with a dilemma because if I got injured, I would not be worth anything to anyone.' While all the other Warriors' internationals found employment elsewhere, together with most of the rest of the squad, Wales's other four regions were not in the market for a hooker and Davies came back from the tour with nowhere to go to. He returned to his old job as an electrical engineer and secured a part-time contract with Neath in the semi-professional Welsh Premier Division. He received less than £10,000 a year from rugby, although he had been offered a far more lucrative contract by one of the leading sides in France, Stade Français.

'It was tempting and I fancied the idea of a move to France, but the stipulation was that I had to retire from international rugby,' said Davies. 'I had only been a professional rugby player for two years having chosen to be part-time because I wanted something in my everyday life which was not connected to rugby, but it became clear to me once I had broken into the Wales squad that I had to devote all my working time to the game. My wife, Angharad, was keen on a move to Paris because the summer months had been difficult for me financially, but I still wanted to play for Wales, even if I knew that my hold on the hooker's jersey would be weakened by playing for a part-time side.'

GRAND SLAM!

His fears came true when he was left out of the side for the first of the four autumn internationals in 2004 against South Africa, being relegated to the bench with the Newport Gwent Dragons' hooker Steve Jones taking over. Davies, who had been first capped by Steve Hansen on the 2002 tour to South Africa, regained his place for the following match against Romania and, after an outstanding display against New Zealand, was offered a contract for the rest of the season by the English Premiership club, Gloucester, whose coach Dean Ryan expressed amazement that a player of Davies's quality had been on the market for so long. Gloucester signed him because of long-term injuries to their senior hookers, the France international Olivier Azam and Chris Fortey, and they had no hesitation in going for Davies even though he was not eligible to play in the Heineken Cup and would be absent for most of the following February and March because of international commitments. 'We were amazed to get him,' said Ryan in an interview with *The Guardian*. 'He is a complete footballer who does his job in the set-pieces and acts as an extra flanker in the loose. He was hugely responsible for Wales's victory over England, and I do not understand how he slipped through the fingers of the Welsh regions.'

Davies's previous visit to Scotland had been in the autumn of 2004 when, taken on as a non-contract player by Neath-Swansea Ospreys, he was selected as a replacement for the Celtic League match against Borders. 'I sat on the bench and got on for the second half, then returned home the following morning to play for Neath against Pontypridd,' he said. 'I could have gone right down: it was hard, but I knew I had to be strong. I kept telling myself never to give up and that things could have been worse. The fact that Wales are doing so well is all the more special to me because of what I went through last year and because it has come so late in my rugby career. For the first time, I've got faith: I play for a superb club where each home game is like an international thanks to our incredible supporters, and I am part of a Wales team which is playing superb rugby.'

Earlier in his career, Davies had been written off as being too small to make the grade at international level as a hooker, but what he lacked in bulk, he more than made up for in heart and in endeavour. Hansen appreciated Davies's honesty and uncomplicated delight at being given his first chance in the international arena three months before his 30th birthday. While Wales were winning plaudits for the breathless effervescence of their rugby, Ruddock's influence on the set-pieces was not receiving the attention it merited: when they played France at the Millennium Stadium in 2004, Wales lost 17 of their 30 scrums and lineouts; in Paris a year later, they won 23 of their 30 set-pieces and reduced France's lineout efficiency to less than 75 per cent.

Set-pieces did not come into it in Murrayfield, so poor was Scotland's grasp of the game's rudiments. After 18 minutes, Wales were leading 24–0, having scored another try which would have had a lustre even in the golden era of the 1970s. Martyn Williams, whose range of skills would not have made him look out of place in the Harlem Globetrotters' basketball side, confounded the defence with a neat reverse pass, Stephen Jones glided through a gap and Shane Williams finished off for his third try of the tournament. Far from being sent home to think again, Wales had confounded the Scots with their speed of thought and execution of plays. It was exhibition stuff.

Scotland stemmed the flow briefly with a Chris Paterson penalty, but Tom Shanklin almost immediately set up Wales's fourth try, charging through the wing Sean Lamont's attempted tackle to free Morgan who scored his second try after a darting break by the scrum-half Dwayne Peel. With Stephen Jones converting all five to supplement a first-quarter penalty, Wales were within sight of their record number of points in a championship match away from home, a landmark set 96 years before when France had been seen off 47–5 in Paris. If mention of the Grand Slam had been banned by Ruddock before, the words were on the lips of every Welsh supporter at Murrayfield. The Wales team manager Alan Phillips gave a half-time television interview in front of the players' tunnel at Murrayfield in which he tried to stress that there was still a lot to play for in the second half, but it was all he could do to keep the smile off his face.

Peel, who was to be voted the man of the match against Scotland for his all-action performance, lifting the pace of the game at moments when the Scots were desperate for a breather, went into the match, in the eyes of many observers, vying with the Scotland scrum-half Chris Cusiter for the Lions' Test jersey against New Zealand the following June. Cusiter cut a forlorn figure when he was replaced three minutes into the second half; while his side was by then well beaten, it had not been a case of the Wales forwards steamrolling over their opposite numbers and dominating possession. The match statistics, compiled by Computacenter, showed that Wales had attempted more tackles than Scotland, 185 compared to 136, and that the Scots had completed more passes, 214 as opposed to 201. Scotland had won possession 123 times in open play, compared to Wales's 78, and made an astonishingly high 77 visits to Wales's 22. The figures were distorted by Scotland's comeback in the second half, when their cause had long been lost, but they also proved Peel's value as his team's catalyst, sensing opportunities when opponents were unaware of danger.

Peel was winning his 40th cap at the age of 23, having first been recognised by Graham Henry in 2001. The Llanelli Scarlets' number 9 had been used as a replacement throughout the 2004 Six Nations by Steve Hansen who, with his pack struggling up front in virtually every match, had preferred the more abrasive Gareth Cooper at scrum-half. Cooper had made his debut three months before Peel, but at the start of the 2005 Six Nations he had won 14 fewer caps than his rival, having missed a number of matches through injury. When he took over from Hansen, Ruddock not only had the luxury of choosing between two scrum-halfs who had both proved themselves at international level, but also had a choice of two players blessed with different strengths. Wales had a long tradition of rivalry at scrum-half: Dicky Owen and Tommy Vile in the 1900s; Bobby Delahay and Wick Powell in the 1920s; Onllwyn Brace and Lloyd Williams in the 1950s; Gareth Edwards and Ray 'Chico' Hopkins at the start of the 1970s; Brynmor Williams and Terry Holmes at the end of the 1970s; while Robert Jones had to see off a number of challengers from the mid-1980s, including David Bishop, Jonathan Griffiths, Chris Bridges, Rupert Moon and Robert Howley. Scrum-half is a position where Wales have traditionally been strong: Hopkins, like the Aberavon scrum-half Clive Shell who also had the misfortune in the 1970s to understudy Edwards, was capped once, a figure which would have been significantly higher had he been available for any other country.

Cooper had not been available for the 2004 summer tour to Argentina and South Africa, and Peel made only his second start since the pre-2003 World Cup friendly against Scotland when he lined up against the Pumas in Tucuman. It gave him an opportunity he was not to squander and when the 2005 Six Nations campaign finished, he had started every match under Ruddock except for the friendly against Japan the previous November. Given their rivalry, it was surprising that as they contemplated who would get the nod for the opening championship match against Ireland, they had never opposed each other in senior rugby. 'We both seem to be injured when our teams play each other,' said Peel. 'We are good friends, and knowing that you have such a good player battling for the jersey keeps you on your toes, which can only be good for the team. Gareth has more pace than me and we are different types of scrum-halfs. I have the advantage of having partnered Stephen Jones at Llanelli for several seasons before he moved to France, but Gareth has partnered him on a number of occasions for Wales and Stephen knows us both well.'

Peel, not surprisingly given the way their styles contrast, is the quieter of the pair. Cooper has a touch of the former scrum-half Sid Going about him, combative and abrasive, a menace around the fringes, while Peel eschews confrontation and lives more off his wits, always keeping opposition back rows interested: his performance at Murrayfield was reminiscent of the way the England scrum-half Matt Dawson had tormented Wales at the Millennium Stadium in the 2001 Six Nations, never missing an opportunity to touch and go and stretch a defence which, from the opening minutes, had struggled to pinpoint the epicentre of England's attack, unsure when or where Dawson was going to pop up. Henry used to rave about Peel, frustrated that in 2001 the Ireland international Guy Easterby was keeping Peel out of the Llanelli team while Cooper was playing, in between injuries, for Bath in the Zurich Premiership. Cooper was not available for the final two matches of the 2005 Six Nations after damaging ankle ligaments playing in the tsunami appeal match between the hemispheres at Twickenham at the beginning of March, leaving Peel to play out the full 80 minutes against Scotland and Ireland.

Peel, who had started the match by upending the Scotland hooker and captain Gordon Bulloch, set up Wales's sixth and final try at Murrayfield, taking a trademark quick penalty to create Rhys Williams's second try. Wales then relaxed visibly, their minds on their fifth and final game. Ireland, whose Grand Slam hopes had ended the previous day after France had won at Lansdowne Road, had the advantage of an extra day's rest and, while the French had exposed the Irish defence, they would certainly ask more questions of ball-carriers than the Scots and they would be able to hold on to possession with considerably more resolve. Given that Wales spent most of the final 30 minutes at Murrayfield defending their line, it was a better rehearsal for the final day than the first half had been. When the final whistle sounded, Scotland had salvaged some face by scoring three tries, two when the second row Brent Cockbain was in the sin-bin after he had been penalised for killing the ball, but there was no gainsaying Wales's overwhelming superiority. The ball had been in play for more than 43 minutes, a championship record; back in 1978 if the ball-in-play time exceeded 20 minutes, it was regarded as a fast, open match.

The Wales players were almost too tired to celebrate afterwards, although Martyn Williams was later to say that they had been surprised at the ease with which they had repeatedly cut open the Scottish defence in the first half. The joy of their achievement – it was the first time Wales had won three consecutive away matches in the championship since 1985 and none of the players had won at Murrayfield before – was all the more pronounced because of where they had come from. 'When you go through bad periods, it makes you appreciate the good times all the more,' said Stephen Jones. 'Two years ago, we were whitewashed in the Six Nations and laughed at: the pain hurt. We have not won anything yet, but we have shown, with the nucleus of the same squad, that we are a good team. It is going to be a crazy week. It is going to be something special and we are fortunate to be a part of it. We are in a great position, but we know we are at the point where we could lose everything.'

The Murrayfield bogey had not just been laid to rest but buried six feet under. In 1973 and 1975, Wales's Grand Slam hopes had come unstuck in Edinburgh. In 1973, they had not lost to Scotland for six years, but they failed to score and were surprisingly overwhelmed at forward. Two years later, having won 25–10 at the Parc des Princes, a world-record crowd of 104,000 (40,000 of them Welsh) had crammed into Murrayfield on St David's Day. There were scenes of chaos around the ground with thousands unable to get in, while hundreds who had squeezed through the turnstiles struggled to get back out because the intense crush on the terraces meant that they could not see anything. After the match, the Scottish Rugby Union made every international at Murrayfield an all-ticket affair and limited the capacity to 71,000. The Wales second row Allan Martin had had the chance to draw the match with a touchline conversion of the flanker Trevor Evans's try, but what turned out to be the final kick of the match drifted wide.

While the Scots and the Welsh were Celtic cousins, the rugby rivalry between the countries had been flavoured with bitterness since the nineteenth century. Even in the early 1990s, when amateurism was in its death throes, the SRU used to bombard the Welsh Rugby Union with letters alleging that the regulations had been infringed in some way. Scotland had refused to play Wales in 1897 after the Welsh Football Union, as the WRU was called in those days, had sanctioned a subscription of 1,000 shillings from Union funds to the testimonial fund set up to mark the retirement of the then Wales captain Arthur 'Monkey' Gould, whose long career had led to him being dubbed rugby union's equivalent of W.G. Grace. The SRU, together with the Rugby Football Union, got the International Rugby Board involved, but the WFU refused to back down and withdrew from the IRB, only to be readmitted the following year after agreeing not to pick Gould in any future internationals. The SRU threatened to cancel fixtures again in

FLAMING RED

1920 because Wales had chosen a professional boxer, Jerry Shea, in their three-quarter line; in 1923, the SRU ordered, under the threat of suspension, the Scottish international Neil McPherson, to hand back his gold watch, which had been presented to every Newport player to mark their invincible season in 1921–22 after a fund had been set up by the club's supporters (the Prince of Wales contributed one shilling); and the SRU showed a complete lack of empathy when Welsh rugby, a victim of the economic downturn suffered by heavy industries, lost a number of players to professional rugby league.

Given the SRU's staunch upholding of the old amateur regulations – the game north of the border had always been regarded as a middle class preserve, whereas in Wales rugby's roots were unmistakably working class – it was not surprising that the onset of professionalism in 1995 led to a steady decline in the game in Scotland, notwithstanding the fact that they won the last Five Nations Championship, in 1999, after Wales had defeated England at Wembley. Two months before Wales's 2005 victory at Murrayfield, Scottish rugby was thrown into turmoil after a number of executives on the SRU resigned in protest at what they claimed was unproductive interference by elected, amateur members of the Union's general committee. The SRU was £20 million in debt and the executives had devised ways of reducing it through methods which trampled on tradition, such as the idea of moving some internationals, including matches in the Six Nations, away from Murrayfield in a bid to widen the game's constituency.

The political infighting which was blighting the Scottish game resembled that which had brought Welsh rugby to its knees a decade earlier. Not that any of Wales's supporters in the crowd at Murrayfield cared as they headed out of the ground and looked forward to their first match for 11 years when there was a Grand Slam at stake. They had witnessed a performance which, in its very different way, had been as ruthless and exploitative of opposition weaknesses as those put on by the three Grand Slam teams of the 1970s. 'We had not started well in our previous three matches and we were determined to get off to a flier today,' said Ryan Jones in the after match press conference. 'We can now look forward to Wales's biggest game for years and it makes a change after a few years in the doldrums. We proved against France that we have the fitness and the physique to compete at this level, while we showed today that we can start a match. If we put it all together, who knows what we will be capable of.'

Wales left Edinburgh for Cardiff that night because they had one day fewer than Ireland to prepare for the showdown between the countries – the Irish still had the Triple Crown and the championship title to aim for – that Saturday. Neutrals were rooting for a team which had set the Six Nations ablaze with its all-action style. In the rewritten words of the song: 'Wales on fire, rolling down the road . . .'

CHAPTER 8

The Green, Green Grass of Home

I thought I would have a quiet pint – and about 17 noisy ones.

Gareth Chilcott

AND THEN THERE WAS ONE. THE COINCIDENCES AND connections with 1983, the last time Wales had defeated Ireland in Cardiff, were plentiful. That year, there was a general election in Britain; at the start of 2005, even before the Six Nations Championship had kicked off, political pundits were predicting that the country would be called to the polls by the early summer; 1983 was the year of a British and Irish Lions tour to New Zealand – as was the case in 2005; one of Wales's try scorers against Ireland in 1983 was the wing Elgan Rees whose daughter, Sarra, was marrying the Ireland and Llanelli Scarlets' flanker Simon Easterby in July 2005; in 1983 the most talked about player in Wales was a Pontypool scrum-half who had resumed his career after breaking his neck at Aberavon the previous season, David Bishop, while the most celebrated player in the country ten weeks into 2005 was Gavin Henson who, it was confirmed after the victory over Ireland, was going out with the singer Charlotte Church; and in 1983 Mike Ruddock was a wing forward in a Swansea team which won the *Western Mail* unofficial club championship for the first time in more years than the vast majority of their supporters could remember, while in 2005 Ruddock was in charge of a Wales team seeking its first Grand Slam in more years than their supporters cared to remember.

Any omen was worth clutching at, in other words, for a nation whose citizens had a reputation for being confident after the event. *The Guardian*, doing its bit to boost the brio of the Welsh, pointed out that it was lucky for Wales when the year had both a two and a five in it: the last time it had occurred, in 1952, they had won the Grand Slam. One of the Wales squad in 2005, the replacement prop John Yapp, had yet to be born when Ireland had last left Cardiff in defeat, and the 22-year unbeaten run by the Irish away to Wales was one of international rugby's most remarkable records: it marked the longest period of time that one team in the championship had ever gone without defeating another at home. It was all the harder to explain because Ireland, like Wales, had spent much of the intervening period in the wilderness; for several years in the 1990s the meeting between the two Celts often ended up deciding the destiny of the wooden spoon. For 18 years from 1984 it had been a fixture the home side had won only twice, on each occasion the team playing on their own soil was Ireland, in 1990 and 1996. Theories abounded as to why home advantage had so often, and so perversely, counted for nothing, but the most plausible was the contention that neither side, during a period when they were unaccustomed to winning, was comfortable with the tag of favourites that tended to be placed around the neck of the team which was playing in front of its own supporters.

Wales had lost 21–9 to Ireland in Cardiff in 1985 after their full-back Mark Wyatt missed six penalties; in 1987, Wales were beaten 15–11 despite scoring two tries in the opening 30 minutes; and two years later, the English referee Roger Quittenton once again 'endeared' himself to Welsh supporters at the National Stadium when he allowed Ireland's winning try to stand. It was scored by the outside-half Paul Dean, the referee having missed a blatant knock-on by the centre David Irwin in the build-up. Quittenton had been the man in the middle in 1978 when Wales had played the All Blacks in Cardiff, having gone 25 years without a victory in the fixture. The drought had seemed to be at an end in the last minute when Wales, in their first international at home since the retirements of Gerald Davies, Phil Bennett and Gareth Edwards, had been leading by two points with one minute to go. A lineout ten metres inside the Wales half led to theatrics normally seen in London's West End; as the ball was thrown in, the New Zealand middle jumper, Andy Haden, dived to the ground as if trying to get out of the way of a charging bull. At the front of the lineout, Haden's second row colleague, Frank Oliver, was also claiming a foul. Quittenton awarded New Zealand a penalty, judging that the Wales second row Geoff Wheel had impeded Oliver. It was only when television replays showed how Haden had cheated that Quittenton became vilified, even though he had arguably made the right decision. Years later Haden admitted that some of the New Zealand players had agreed that, should they find themselves losing by a couple of points towards the end of the game, they would look to earn a penalty by cheating, while 15 years on, in 1993, Oliver conceded that Wheel had probably been harshly penalised.

Quittenton refused to speak to the media after Irwin's

unpunished knock-on helped his side to a 19–13 victory, and it was the last time the Englishman took charge of a Wales international. In 1991 Wales ended their three-match losing run to Ireland, but were outscored by four tries to two in a 21–21 draw; in 1993, a year which had started with a 10–9 victory over England, Ireland won a poor game 19–14; in 1995 a 16–12 defeat condemned Wales to the wooden spoon; in 1997 Ireland set a new championship record after their 26–25 victory marked their seventh consecutive match without defeat in Cardiff; a change of scene did nothing for Wales in 1999 when they lost 29–23 at Wembley; in 2001 Ireland's first appearance at the Millennium Stadium saw them cruise home 36–6; and in 2003 Ronan O'Gara's late, late drop goal sent Wales on their way to another whitewash-coated wooden spoon.

The words disaster and tragedy had on numerous occasions been inappropriately applied to Wales's tale of woe between 1988 and the arrival of Graham Henry in the Principality ten years later, but two of the ever-presents in Wales's 2005 Grand Slam side, the second row Brent Cockbain and the flanker Martyn Williams, were able to accept misfortune on the rugby field for what it was: a set-back which did not mean that the sun would fail to rise the following morning. 'I think sports followers sometimes let their emotions run away with them,' said the former England full-back Alastair Hignell, a victim of multiple sclerosis at the end of the 1990s, whose late missed penalty at Twickenham in 1978 sent Wales on their way to their third Grand Slam in seven years. 'I used to receive scores of abusive letters from fans: I remember one which branded me as the most disgraceful player ever to pull on an England shirt. Letting off steam gives people a release, but we should never forget the fact that it is only sport, even if players at the top level are now professionals. It is not the end of the world when things go wrong.'

THE GREEN, GREEN GRASS OF HOME

In September 2000 Williams had just turned 25 when his 18-year-old brother, Craig, was diagnosed with skin cancer. Craig died three months later. 'When I look at the papers and see nice things written about me, I try hard not to get too excited,' said Williams. 'I know from experience that life is so up and down. Craig had seemed fine the summer before his death. When he was told he had cancer he did not ask how long he had left. My parents and I knew that it was only a matter of months. It was tough, but I guess that is one of the good things about playing rugby; you can pour out a lot of frustration and anger in training. It helps clear the mind. It got difficult towards the end when Craig was in a hospice. My club, Cardiff, were very understanding and gave me time off. For a couple of weeks I stayed completely away from rugby. That helped, and we are OK now as a family. But you never totally recover from something like that. Craig has been a constant source of inspiration to me throughout my career. When I led the team out on to the Millennium Stadium against England for my 50th cap, I dedicated that special moment to him.'

Cockbain won his first cap for Wales against Romania in 2003 six days after his wife, Kate, had given birth to their first child, a son they named Toby. In the summer of 2004, Toby was diagnosed with a brain tumour. He died at the family home that September. He was just over a year old. 'Returning to the rugby field was hard because you cannot just bounce back from something like that,' said Cockbain. 'After what I went through with Toby's diagnosis and the loss of his life, I know that this is just a game of rugby and there are more important things in life.' He was speaking after the Grand Slam had been secured, a bottle of beer in one hand and a sense of perspective in the other. 'Pretty much the worst thing that can happen to a parent is to lose a child, so rugby is really a piece of piss now. I do not get as nervous before games as I used to.' The Cockbains help raise funds for

Latch (the children's leukaemia charity), through the Toby Lloyd Cockbain Foundation that they set up in memory of their son. Gavin Henson donated the boots he had worn against England for an auction at a charity dinner organised by Kate Cockbain the following month. They raised £8,500.

Ireland were confident they could impose themselves physically on Wales. Less than one minute had gone when their hooker, Shane Byrne, tried it on after a lineout. He found Cockbain waiting, fists clenched. Wales were not going to be pushed around. Seven minutes later, Cockbain charged down a kick by the Ireland captain Brian O'Driscoll and the pair fell to the ground. As O'Driscoll got up, he used Cockbain's head as a lever, pushing it into the ground. The Wales second row grabbed the left boot of O'Driscoll who, after eventually forcing its release, brought his right foot down on Cockbain's hip. The incident, which happened off the ball, was missed by the match officials. The citing commissioner chose not to take any action against the Irish captain, although he did call the Ireland second row Paul O'Connell to account for a second-half punch on his opposite number Robert Sidoli, and the lock was subsequently banned for two weeks.

Ruddock had again been unable to field an unchanged side. The wing Rhys Williams had sustained a calf strain at Murrayfield the previous Sunday and, although he was named in the side, he had been forced to withdraw on the day before the Ireland game. His replacement at Murrayfield, Hal Luscombe, had failed to recover from a hamstring strain and Mark Taylor, who had only ever started in the centre in his 48-cap career, was chosen on the right wing. It was his first appearance in the 2005 Six Nations. Sonny Parker, who had missed the first four matches because of a neck injury, was named on the bench. Ruddock delayed making the changes public until shortly before the kick-off, not wishing to alert the Irish who, had they known in advance that a centre was playing out of position on the wing, might have adjusted their tactics to take advantage.

'We knew all week that it was going to be touch and go with Rhys and Hal as far as starting the game went,' said Ruddock. 'I was hoping that one of them would have pulled through and Tayls would have slipped in on the bench. When we got the word the day before the game that neither would make it, I kept it quiet because I did not want Ireland to pick up on it. I chose Tayls on the wing because I did not want to break up the centre partnership of Gavin Henson and Tom Shanklin, particularly against O'Driscoll and Kevin Maggs. Tayls had not played much rugby since the turn of the year and to put him straight into the centre would not have been fair on him. I was very confident in his ability and he did an exceptional job on the wing. It said everything for the squad of players we had that although we were down to the bare bones after suffering so many injuries, we finished the campaign off in style.'

The 31-year-old Taylor was the longest serving player in the Wales squad, having made his debut against South Africa in November 1994. The previous December he had found himself in hospital after developing an eye infection when he suffered a bout of chicken pox. 'I wondered if my career was over,' he said. 'I could never have imagined as I lay in my hospital bed that I would be part of a Grand Slam winning team a few months later.' When he recovered from his illness in the new year, Taylor struggled to regain his place in the Llanelli Scarlets' midfield. He wanted to sign a short-term contract with an English club, but his region refused to release him because they still had to seal Heineken Cup qualification for the following season. His only meaningful action before the Ireland international had come at the beginning of the month when he had taken part in the tsunami appeal fund-raising match between the two hemispheres at Twickenham. Taylor's elevation marked an eerie coincidence. Just before Wales's Grand Slam decider against France in Cardiff in 1978, Gerald Davies withdrew from the side because of injury. His place was taken by Gareth Evans, who played his rugby for Newport in the centre. It was the only change made by Wales in their entire championship campaign that year.

Ruddock was forced, because of injuries, to start with four different right wings during the 2005 Six Nations: Hal Luscombe, Kevin Morgan, Rhys Williams and Taylor; he used three different blind-side flankers, Dafydd Jones, Jonathan Thomas and Ryan Jones, but key combinations survived through the whole tournament. The centres, the half-backs and the front five remained the same and the players who did come in entered a winning environment. Confidence and understanding blossomed and, far from being nervous at the moment of reckoning against Ireland, Wales were composed, assertive and bold, ready for their day of destiny, producing what was to be their most complete performance of the championship.

It was a day which had started the moment the final whistle had sounded at Murrayfield the previous Sunday. The *Western Mail* devoted at least six of its news pages to rugby throughout the week, although the *Daily Post*, which served North Wales, did not get quite as carried away by nationalistic fervour, preferring to concentrate on the travails of Wales's football team. The atmosphere was far more heady than it had appeared to be in 1988, the last time Wales had gone for the Grand Slam in Cardiff; even though it was then ten years since the feat had been achieved, England had not yet emerged as a force in the game. There were those who believed that fortune was cyclical, pointing out that Wales's three golden eras had followed lean times. It was different in 2005: England had by then broken Wales's record for the number of Grand Slam successes, they had won the World Cup and they had a club game which, in terms of intensity and support, resembled Welsh club rugby up to end of the 1980s; the game in Wales, in contrast, had entered its deepest ever period of decline, worse even than the 1920s when a depressed economy had made players susceptible to the entreaties and cash treats of rugby league clubs.

The growth of rugby in Wales in the late nineteenth century had coincided with a heady economic boom. 'The period between 1880 and 1900 saw some 200,000 people move into Glamorgan alone,' wrote David Smith and Gareth Williams in *Fields of Praise*. 'It was the greatest industrial explosion Wales had ever seen. The last third of the century saw the emergence of a new Welsh nationality. Wales came to be regarded as a distinct entity. The Welsh Rugby Union would have a distinct role to play in the new chapter that was opening in the history of Wales, a Wales characterised not only by self-awareness, but a wider awareness: the transport revolution brought Wales closer to England as well as bringing together parts of Wales itself . . . As the Welsh economy took off, so also did Welsh rugby football.' Wales's victory over the New Zealand team in 1905, they argued, firmly established that rugby union had become the national sport of Wales.

Rugby union's status as Wales's national sport has long been disputed. Writing in the *Western Mail* five days after the victory over Ireland, the columnist Aled Blake argued that the Grand Slam success would have no impact for Wales on the global stage. 'Let's face it, the fact is that barely any country worth its salt has a clue about the sport of rugby,' he wrote. 'BBC Wales said one million people tuned in to watch the match. Which leaves two million Welshmen and women who didn't watch it at all, and probably, like me, didn't give a monkey's. We are the silent majority who think Wales has a hell of a lot more to be proud of than its rugby team. We think measuring our nationality against some two-bit sports team is not something we need to do.'

Blake missed the point, in the manner of other football followers who have through the ages decried rugby union's perceived popularity. You did not have to be a lover of rugby union in order to bask in the glow of the feel-good factor which had been generated by the success of Ruddock's side. An estimated 200,000 people descended on Cardiff on the day of the Ireland international; a big screen was erected outside Cardiff City Hall, a few hefty punts away from the Millennium Stadium, where tens of thousands craned their necks to get a view of the action. They joined in the rendition of '*Hen Wlad fy Nhadau*', which was led at the ground by the singers Charlotte Church and Katherine Jenkins. The song had been adopted as Wales's national anthem after the 1905 rugby international against New Zealand in Cardiff: the Welsh players sang it as a response to the All Blacks' haka and the crowd joined in the chorus. 'The song had been around for some 50 years, composed in 1856 by Evan and James James of Pontypridd, father and son,' said David Smith. 'It was given its first official airing in 1905 and the response of the crowd meant that it soon became the national anthem.' A game which gave a country its anthem is entitled to regard itself as its national sport, but more than that, throughout the years, successes on the international rugby field had fuelled national pride: in what other sphere was success over England so regular?

When Wales lost the 1987 World Cup semi-final to New Zealand by an embarrassing 49–6, their then manager Clive Rowlands proclaimed: 'Well, we can always go back to beating England every year.' It was not the smartest of remarks to make given the gaping gulf which had opened up between two of the sport's biggest traditional rivals, but you knew where Rowlands was coming from. More men in Wales may have played soccer than rugby union, but the national football side had never been among the leading countries in the world, indeed they were regarded as a perennial makeweight. Welsh football might have mined great individuals, but it was Welsh rugby which produced great teams. Rugby union was something that Wales had traditionally been good at, pioneers throughout the ages, and its roots were solidly working class, unlike the game in the other three home unions. It was the sport of the masses, and while Blake could point out that George Bush would hardly have made a vow to tighten the United States' economic links with Wales after the Grand Slam success (no more than he would have had Wales won the football World Cup), any American trying to fight their way down Queen Street or St Mary Street in Cardiff on 19 March 2005 would have been interested to know what was going on, before returning home to relate the tale.

And what a tale! Wales had started the year as long shots to win the Grand Slam and local bookmakers were preparing themselves for a battering. The television weather presenter Sian Lloyd had placed a £100 bet on Wales to win the title at odds of 16–1; her investment looked sound. Ireland had to beat Wales by more than 13 points to win the championship. France were also in contention, although if Wales lost by fewer than 13 points, the French would need to run up a cricket score against Italy in Rome to retain their crown. It was not just the title Wales were after: it was all about the Grand Slam. In 1994, when Wales had gone to Twickenham looking for a clean sweep only to lose to England, it had seemed anti-climactic when their captain Ieuan Evans climbed the steps to receive the Five Nations trophy: they had won and lost at the same time, with the players not knowing whether to celebrate or to weep.

The crowds had arrived in Cardiff early. By nine-thirty, long queues outside popular bars had started snaking around corners. Ticket touts had risen with the dawn chorus and were asking for extortionate sums. Hordes of Irish supporters were in town, confident of their side's long unbeaten record in Cardiff continuing. Green mingled with red and, standing incongruously outside a bookshop in the Hayes, was a man sporting an England rugby jersey. The shelves in the sports section of the shop were lined with books celebrating England's recent successes: the faces of Sir Clive Woodward, Martin Johnson, Jonny Wilkinson, Jason Robinson, Matt Dawson and Will Greenwood beamed out. The few volumes on Welsh rugby were of an earlier vintage: the second autobiographies of 1970s legends mingled with works on the 1950s: silver hair compared to silverware. 'Unhappy the land that needs heroes,' the German playwright Bertolt Brecht had written. Unhappier the land that had none.

Inside the ground, as the kick-off drew near, the entertainer Max Boyce came on to the pitch to do a turn. He had achieved prominence in Britain in the 1970s through an album entitled *Live at Treorchy*, a humorous, musical homage to the Wales team and players of the time. One of his numbers, 'Hymns and Arias', came to be adopted by crowds at the National Stadium, while other song titles, such as the 'Fly-Half Factory' and the 'Pontypool Front Row', became neologisms. If Boyce had come to personify that golden era – failure does not lend itself to humour, unlike success – he, along with the national team, had been reborn. He was the man for the occasion and the decision to hire him that day was a masterstroke: he was a symbol of the 1970s who did not invite comparisons with the current crop of players and, as he sang verses of 'Hymns and Arias', which he had rewritten to encompass the present, the crowd joined in with the unchanged chorus. Boyce, on a day which was the biggest in the careers of each and every one of the Wales players, lightened the tension in the crowd. Wales ran out to a sea of smiling faces. Boyce, not history nor the enormity of the moment, had set the tone.

The Irish had celebrated St Patrick's Day two days earlier and the green army was hoping for rain to help put out Wales's fire. 'When we awoke on the Saturday morning, pulled back the curtains in our bedrooms and saw the sun was shining in a clear blue sky, we knew it was going to be our day,' said Gavin Henson. 'Ireland are quite an old side and the weather meant we could play it fast and open. Our high-tempo game has been the key to the Grand Slam and at no stage did I think we would lose to the Irish.' It was truly like an early summer's day, and as members of the Welsh Rugby Union took their seats, they held their hands in front of their faces: not, as might have been the case not that long before, to hide their identities, but to keep the sun out of their eyes.

After the anthems had been sung (it was just as well that the sliding Millennium Stadium roof had not been closed because the noise generated by the rendition of '*Hen Wlad fy Nhadau*' would have blown a huge hole through it), Wales kicked off. The Ireland number 8 Anthony Foley received the ball in his own 22 and set off on a bullocking run which covered 30 metres. The Irish played for position, keeping it tight as Wales knew they would, and took the lead when Ronan O'Gara kicked a 25-metre penalty. Stephen Jones had the chance to equalise with a 40-metre penalty after O'Driscoll had been pulled up for using his hands in a ruck – although the officials had missed Gethin Jenkins treading on the back of the Llanelli Scarlets' flanker Simon Easterby, who had been lying on the wrong side of the ball – but the Wales fly-half dragged it wide. The Ireland players rushed to congratulate the centre Kevin Maggs after he had ended a Wales attack by upending Henson.

Ireland had started the stronger, but Wales were not betraying

any sign of nerves. In each of their previous matches, someone
had stepped up to the plate at the vital moment and, as he had
done on Wales's previous appearance at the ground, against
England six weeks before, Henson seized the moment. A Wales
attack was going nowhere when the ball came back to Henson
who was standing 40 metres from the Irish line, dead in front of
the posts. He dropped for goal as the Ireland prop Reggie
Corrigan bore down on him: as the ball was going past the
Irishman, it brushed his fingertips. Corrigan appeared to have
succeeded only in diverting it towards the posts, but Henson
maintained: 'It was going over anyway, but things like that help
make it your day.'

It was not to be Ireland fly-half Ronan O'Gara's day. He had
started the Six Nations as the pretender to the Lions' outside-half
crown, should Jonny Wilkinson fail to recover from injury before
the tour to New Zealand that summer, but the Munsterman had
been overtaken by Stephen Jones. Wales were attacking on
Ireland's ten-metre line when Tom Shanklin, making his one
blemish of the afternoon, was robbed of the ball by O'Driscoll. It
was fed out to O'Gara who looked to the right-hand touchline and
aimed to kick. O'Gara had moved to the side to give himself a
better body position for the kick, and that gave the prop Gethin
Jenkins the extra half a second he needed to bear down on the fly-
half. O'Gara kicked with a low trajectory and Wales had spent
time on the training field working out ways of charging down his
kicks. As Jenkins pounced, O'Gara could not withdraw from the
kick and the ball ricocheted off the prop towards Ireland's 22,
which had been left unguarded because the full-back Geordan
Murphy had joined the backline. Jenkins hacked the ball towards
the Ireland line, hoping that it would not stop just short, forcing
him to bend down to pick it up and run the risk of a knock-on. It
had just enough momentum and Jenkins did not panic, waiting

and evaluating before acting, and Wales were ahead. O'Gara, in the act of stepping over Jenkins, caught the footballing prop's shoulder with a boot and Jenkins hurled the ball at him before being mobbed by his colleagues.

Jenkins revealed afterwards that he had played a lot of football as a teenager. 'Michael Owen and I used to play for age-group sides at Pontyclun,' he said. 'We thought we were alright until we played a team from Cardiff one day: they had a little kid who ran rings round us and scored four goals.' That little kid had grown into the Wales and West Bromwich Albion striker Robert Earnshaw who, not long after Jenkins had claimed his try, was to score a hat-trick in the Premiership match at Charlton Athletic. 'I don't think O'Gara saw me coming,' said Jenkins. 'Once I had charged it down it was a case of "Hold on": it was uncharted territory for me. I had to kick it on; there was no way I could pick it up. I was telling myself not to kick it dead and was trying to keep it under control. The few seconds it took for the ball to bounce over the try-line seemed to go on forever: I could feel someone running behind me and it was a relief when I was able to fall on the ball. I used to love playing football, more so than rugby, but the match against Earnshaw showed me that I was a bit too big and slow for soccer and rugby took over when I was 16.'

Stephen Jones's conversion put Wales 10–3 ahead and they were never to look back. Henson stretched the lead in the 25th minute with an even longer kick than the one he had landed against England. Ireland had been penalised at a ruck close to Wales's ten-metre line. As the referee Chris White told the Irish exactly why they had been blown up, Henson stole an extra couple of yards without being detected: it was exactly what the Leicester full-back Tim Stimpson had done in the final minute of the Heineken Cup semi-final against Llanelli at Nottingham Forest's City Ground in 2002 when, much to the fury of the

Scarlets, the ball bounced over off the cross-bar to take the Tigers through to the final. Henson showed the same wisdom of the streets, doing exactly what his predecessors in the 1970s would have done, and his kick also went over only after hitting the woodwork, in his case the left-hand post. Had he taken the 55-metre kick from the actual mark, it is possible that it would have hit the other side of the post and bounced dead.

Wales were 13–3 ahead and Ireland knew they had to hit back immediately. O'Driscoll, who battled manfully all afternoon to find holes in the Welsh defence only to find himself closely policed by Henson and Shanklin, sparked a dangerous attack which saw Denis Hickie fly down his opposite wing. Ireland could not match Wales's attacking zip in broken play and, as they had done for most of the championship, relied on set-plays. This one was out of the top drawer and the Wales full-back Kevin Morgan found himself having to cover Hickie rather than the right wing Girvan Dempsey, who was running on the outside in support. Hickie delayed his pass slightly, but as Dempsey came inside he appeared destined to score, until Stephen Jones, the outside-half who had started Wales's revival in Paris with a jinking break from his own 22, stopped the Irishman just short of the line and waited for his cavalry to arrive.

Ireland had helped themselves to a few of Wales's early lineouts and they had exerted pressure in the scrums, but they looked the more nervous of the two sides, as if they appreciated the importance of making every visit to the Wales 22 count. The second row Malcolm O'Kelly, arguably their best forward that Six Nations, gave away a stupid penalty at a lineout ten metres from the Welsh line when he barged into the Wales second row Robert Sidoli, even though he knew the ball was not going to go anywhere near him. Murphy then kicked the ball out on the full and when Ireland had a scrum 12 metres in front of Wales's try-line, the ball shot off their hooker Shane Byrne's foot and back out of the tunnel and Ireland ended up deep in their own half. Stephen Jones used the territory to land his first penalty of the afternoon after Ireland had handled in a ruck, though O'Gara reduced Wales's half-time lead to 16–6 with a 45-metre penalty in the 37th minute. The atmosphere even got to the referee who forgot to blow for half-time, apologising to his fourth official after allowing Ireland to put into a scrum even though time had run out.

Wales may not have shown the breathless style which had blown away Scotland and Italy, but they were controlled and composed and it was Ireland who had been hustled into making errors. The Irish needed to make a strong start to the second half, but three minutes after the restart they found themselves even further behind when Jones landed his second penalty after Ireland's backs had strayed offside. When O'Gara then missed from 48 metres, the prospects of an Ireland comeback looked slim. Wales went for the kill and had worked an overlap when the ball was moved along the right. Martyn Williams was in the line, but he took his eye off the ball and dropped the pass, a rare lapse by him. It was not an expensive mistake because soon after that Jones kicked his third penalty: Wales were 22–6 ahead and surely not even Ireland, at their home from home, were going to come back from such a large deficit.

Wales's forwards by now were giving as good as they received and the *coup de grâce* was applied by a player who had spent most of the previous two years recovering from operations, Kevin Morgan. Wales took play through a couple of phases, Martyn Williams keeping the move alive with a dive pass Gareth Edwards would have been proud of, and Shanklin ran the smartest of angles into Ireland's 22 before straightening up. The Shanklin of a couple of years before would probably have tried to score the try himself, but, as part of a side playing heads-up rugby, he knew someone would be in support and committed the defence before freeing Morgan, who had an unopposed run to the line for a try which said everything about Ruddock's Wales: flair, pace, awareness and unselfishness.

Jones's conversion made it 29–6 with 20 minutes to go and Wales were dining on heaven's bread once more. Ireland made a flurry of substitutions and the replacement prop Marcus Horan plunged over for their first try. Jones's fourth penalty steadied any nerves among the home supporters, rendering Murphy's try four minutes from time a mere consolation, although it prompted the first sign of nerves among the Wales players. 'I looked at the scoreboard and saw they were only 12 points behind with a few minutes to go,' said the Wales captain Michael Owen. 'Ireland are a quality side and I knew they had it in them to score two quick tries. They had brought on fresh legs, and I think at that stage we were feeling the effects of the game in Scotland six days before when the ball had seemed to be in play forever. We had come so far that we were not going to lose it at the very end. We put our bodies on the line and to hear that final whistle was pure joy. Two years before we had been labelled the worst Wales team in history: then people ignored the fact that we had played some good rugby in defeat. Winning makes all the difference to what the public thinks of you. Our performance against Ireland may not have been our most eye-catching of the year, but it was our best all-round display. It was a massive occasion, but we were not overawed by it. I hope this is the start of something special.'

It may have been Wales's ninth Grand Slam, but it was their first in the professional era. The final whistle, after Martyn Williams, who 48 hours later was voted the man of the tournament, had fittingly had the last of the action when he kicked the ball into touch, was the cue for unrestrained celebration. Unlike 1978, spectators were prevented from getting on to the pitch and the players were able to milk the moment. With no steps up to the directors' box at the Millennium Stadium, a platform had to be erected for Owen and the injured Wales captain Gareth Thomas to receive the Six Nations trophy. As champagne corks popped, a row had broken out among the press photographers. They had been told that precious few passes were being handed out to allow them on to the pitch to get close-up shots of the presentation and celebrations. Wales were suddenly in demand and commercial opportunities beckoned.

When television cameramen asked to be allowed into the Wales dressing-room to film the players in their first moments of private contemplation, they were asked to hand over £1,000 in cash; they beat a hasty retreat. For the first time in 11 years, Wales had become the centre of the rugby media's attention in the final week of a championship. Ruddock had seemed overwhelmed by the presence of so many unfamiliar faces at his media conference the previous Wednesday. His normal routine was to take questions at a top table before going round to speak to different huddles of reporters representing morning, evening and Sunday newspapers, as well as radio and television journalists. The morning papers represented the biggest single group, and as Ruddock stood in the middle of them, he struggled to work out where all the questions were coming from, with his hearing impaired in one ear. He sometimes replied to a questioner by looking at someone else, grateful when the last question was asked so he could slip out of the room.

The players had all been relaxed during the 45-minute session. A smile never left the face of Stephen Jones, who was to be one of three best men at his former Llanelli Scarlets' colleague Simon Easterby's wedding the following July. 'He had better not leave any marks on me on Saturday, otherwise I will embellish a few stories about him in my best man's speech,' he said. Asked whether he was feeling nervous, Jones replied: 'We are where we want to be. Why should we be nervous? After what we have been through in the last few years, this feels like heaven.'

The following day, with the achievement still to sink in, Ruddock had already started to think about the future. 'My aim is to make sure that this team is peaking by the time the 2007 World Cup starts,' he said. 'Everyone wants to try to win the World Cup, so there will be a lot more work going into this side from the coaches. We have a young squad and there is still more to come from the players. The Wales Under-21s won their Grand Slam on the eve of our match against Ireland and those players will be pushing for places in our set-up very soon. By 2007, we should have a very strong group to choose from. The players know that if they drop their standards we are going to get knocked over; our new challenge will be coping with the tag of being the team everyone wants to beat. The fact that they won the Grand Slam after going through some tough times should ensure that no one's feet leave the ground. The players deserve the credit for this success: they are the ones who make the tackles, catch and pass the ball, kick the goals, score the tries, put their heads in the scrum and clear out the rucks. As coaches we can only do so much and our main task is to create an environment where the players are happy, somewhere in which they feel comfortable.'

The week had started with the former England coach Dick Best, part of the Lions' coaching team on the 1993 tour to New Zealand, urging Woodward, the head coach on the 2005 summer trip to the land of the long white cloud, not to become intoxicated by Wales's free-flowing style. Best, who was known as Sulphuric in his coaching days, had claimed that Wales would weaken the Lions because the foundations of their game were built on sand. He had questioned Henson's bottle and had said that he would pick the 36-year-old former England flanker Neil Back, who had retired from international rugby in 2004, ahead of Martyn Williams 'any day of the week'. His remarks provoked outrage in Wales and provided Ruddock with his team-talk. Best had a point: there had been little to suggest during the Six Nations that the Lions would be able to assemble a tight five capable of grinding down the All Blacks, but he failed to acknowledge that two of the architects of that foundation, Graham Henry and Steve Hansen, were back in New Zealand and formed two-thirds of the All Blacks' coaching team. Before Wales's match against Ireland, Woodward, showing a sense of humour he is not usually given enough credit for, wished Ruddock well and said: 'Do you know that I have appointed Dick Best as the chairman of the Lions' selectors?'

On the day that Best was stirring up patriotic fervour in Wales, the Welsh political journalist, Alan Watkins, was arguing in *The Independent* that there was a disposition to 'endow the late 1970s with a glamour which they did not possess at the time . . . If the players of the 1970s were less slick in their passing, they were harder, not in the sense that they were fitter or stronger, but because they were tougher mentally. They would not have allowed Scotland to win a second half 19–8.' Best and Watkins were making essentially the same point, but would the Welsh teams of the 1970s have come back from 15–3 down in Paris? Wales's away record in the Five Nations that decade was not overly impressive, 11 victories in 19 matches; it was at home where they were invincible with 19 wins and a draw in their 20 championship games.

Wales's lack of firepower up front had been overstated. Ireland did not pose anywhere near the problems at forward that they had the previous year in Dublin. While Wales's scrum creaked initially in Paris, it had become immoveable by the end: when the French, needing a converted try to win the game, had a series of five-metre scrums in the final minutes, they got nowhere. 'We were not intimidated by anybody,' said the prop Adam Jones, the one player in the side, apart from the flanker Ryan Jones, who did not owe a debt of gratitude to Hansen, who used to take him off after 30 minutes on the grounds that the prop lacked the necessary match fitness. 'People were concerned about our front five, but we did our job and provided the ball for the likes of Gavin Henson and Shane Williams to do their stuff. We fronted up and I was just glad not to be hauled off half an hour into every game, as I was under Hansen. It started in the 2003 World Cup match against New Zealand, and the worst thing was that I was not given any warning. When it happened against England in the quarter-final, I thought, "Here we go again." I am no fitter than I was a year ago and my fitness test results are the same: the only difference is that we have a new coach who has brought with him a change of ideas.'

The player the media most wanted to talk to was Henson. As reporters waited for him at the foot of the stairs which led to the dressing-rooms at the Millennium Stadium, Charlotte Church was ushered through a door marked private. 'The Welsh Posh and Becks,' said one journalist. *The Guardian* had interviewed the publicist Max Clifford during the week. 'Henson has to be careful that he doesn't get sucked into the media game,' said Clifford. 'Church has more to gain from any relationship. She understands playing the media, even though she is very young. She is more advanced than him in that respect and it is much too early to say if they will become the new Posh and Becks.' Henson had not had any commercial deals before the start of the Six Nations but, according to his agent, Peter Underhill, the penalty against England had kicked his client into the global market. 'There is a huge amount of interest in Gavin and we are negotiating with various parties,' said Underhill. 'All the attention will not change Gavin because he is level-headed and has his feet on the ground.'

THE GREEN, GREEN GRASS OF HOME

Henson duly descended the stairs, dressed in his dinner jacket with the players about to be taken by coach to the post-match dinner at a hotel opposite Cardiff Castle: he was to leave the hotel in a car, with Church sitting next to him on the back seat, a photographer ready to capture the moment. 'We deserved to win the Six Nations because we played the best rugby,' he said. 'Most teams concentrate on defence, but we don't. We concentrate on scoring tries. Beating England was massive for us because it gave us the confidence and belief to go on. I hope there is better to come for this team: the World Cup is a fair way off, but that is what we are building towards.' And then he was off, with no one daring to ask whether he was going to get to the Church on time.

The Ireland players had left the ground long before any of the Welsh players had changed. 'It was a day you did not want to end,' said Mark Taylor. 'I could not take my eyes off the trophy in the dressing-room: there had been a time when I thought I would never be in a position to grab hold of it. When you have been through so many dark periods [Taylor played in Wales's 96–13 defeat against South Africa in 1998], you savour this all the more. I wandered around the changing-room not wanting to shower because it would have meant taking off my jersey. I had thought about retiring after the 2003 World Cup, but now they will have to retire me. I am one cap away from 50 and will do everything I can to get there. You keep yourself so fit in the professional game that it seems silly to call it a day when you are still feeling good. I will hang around and see what happens.'

The coach journey from the ground to the hotel where the dinner was being held would ordinarily have taken between three and four minutes, depending on traffic lights, but Welsh supporters lined the route up Westgate Street, into Castle Street and up Kingsway. Four years before, after Wales had lost 44–15 to England at the Millennium Stadium, supporters had banged their fists on the team coach as it was being driven to the same hotel. Players turned away from the windows or hid their faces behind curtains, not wanting to see the contorted rage on the faces of those who, a few hours earlier, had been cheering them on.

'It had taken us a while to get out of the dressing-room because all the players' families had come in after we had showered and changed,' said Gethin Jenkins. 'We had a photograph taken on the pitch when we were in our tuxedos. When we eventually made our way to the dinner, it was nuts on the way there. People were lining the streets, banging on the bus and waving. There were hundreds of supporters waiting outside the hotel for us and we had to sneak in through the back door.'

The party in Cardiff raged into the long night. More than 60 council workers had spent the early hours of Sunday trying to clear the mountain of rubbish from the city's streets while another 25 had to remove the mess outside the City Hall where an estimated 20,000 fans had watched the match on a big screen. The rubbish was knee-deep in parts and the council admitted that it could have done with more hands. Hoteliers and publicans were counting their takings, with one landlord saying that he had taken as much in one day, £50,000, as it would normally take him two weeks to do. Cardiff was celebrating the 100th anniversary of its being granted city status while it had been made the Welsh capital 50 years before.

With a general election expected to be called within two months, politicians were not slow to jump on the bandwagon, and there were calls for an open-top bus parade to be held in the city as soon as it could be arranged. 'I'd like to use this result as much as I can,' said the First Minister of Wales, Rhodri Morgan, in a column in *The Guardian* on the Monday after the victory. He talked about rising exports, higher inward investment, a boom in tourism and a flood of overseas students being attracted to Wales, and made a few political points before talking about the rugby. The WRU chairman David Pickering said, quite properly, that any celebration of the Grand Slam should embrace the areas geographically covered by Wales's four regions, and not just Cardiff, but the WRU in the end opted, for the sake of convenience, for an all-ticket extravaganza at the Millennium Stadium at the beginning of May when all the squad would be present.

The WRU, as it considered ways to financially exploit Wales's first real success for 27 years, was entitled to ask where Morgan and his Welsh Assembly had been a few years before when the Union, admittedly then run by amateurs rather than executives, had been brought to the brink of bankruptcy because of the crippling debts incurred by the construction of the Millennium Stadium. Politicians had complained when the WRU disbanded Celtic Warriors, the region which had served the Ogwr, Garw and Rhondda Valleys, in May 2004, ostensibly for economic reasons, but had offered no assistance.

Three days after the victory over Ireland, the Wales and former Warriors' hooker Mefin Davies's wife, Angharad, gave birth to their first child, a girl. Davies said he would have pulled out of the match had his wife gone into labour at a crucial time on the day of the game. A new arrival after the rebirth of the game in Wales.

CHAPTER 9

Will You Still Love Me Tomorrow?

*. . . But does he know, does he really know
What he's taken on?*

Gerry Rafferty

EIGHT DAYS AFTER WALES HAD DEFEATED IRELAND TO
secure the Grand Slam, Bristol entertained Exeter in a First
Division match which would have a considerable bearing on who
finished at the top of the table and in line for a place in the Zurich
Premiership. Professional club rugby in England had become
notable for its intensity rather than its creative edge: in the
2004–05 season, player burn-out and concern over the number of
long-term injuries being sustained by players were major issues.
The club game was booming with season-ticket sales at record
levels and sold out signs regularly appearing outside grounds, but
the rugby was rarely stimulating.

When Bristol were relegated from the Premiership in May

2003, the club lost virtually all its senior players and had to start over again on a drastically reduced budget. The former England captain Richard Hill was brought in as the club's director of rugby: Hill had led England against Wales in Cardiff in 1987, one of four players subsequently dropped by the Rugby Football Union for their part in the unseemly scenes which blighted that afternoon. Hill had preceded Mike Ruddock as a coach at Ebbw Vale and at Rodney Parade, Newport, before taking charge at Bristol and he brought back to England with him some of the ways of the Welsh.

'A lot of people have asked me about how surprised I was to see the Welsh team take the Grand Slam,' said Hill. 'I have to say that I've seen it bubbling over the last few years and it did not come as a great shock. When I coached over there, they played with a lot more expression than the English "one out bash" approach. Their forwards had the skills in handling terms, but they lacked the physicality to win enough ball. They have improved their conditioning over the last four years so that they are now able to compete with the big English, Irish and French packs. I think the bonus points system they introduced some years ago has also clearly increased the incentive to score tries and attack is now intrinsically part of their game. Also, from a logistical point of view, it is a lot easier for Mike Ruddock to get his squad together compared to his English counterpart; the more time you have with your players, the more you can develop that club mentality.'

Watching Bristol against Exeter was almost like reliving Wales's Six Nations campaign. Exeter were one-dimensional, over-committing to the breakdown and ripe for the counter-attack. Just as Wales had done against Scotland at Murrayfield, so Bristol had virtually killed the game before the end of the first half thanks to two tries that were the product of moves which originated in their own half. Within 24 hours of Wales beating Ireland to secure their first Grand Slam since 1978, Ruddock had been asked whether he would be flattered by imitation after having devised a style of play which had confounded even the most organised of defences; a style which was all the more refreshing because rugby union had become almost like a 30-man sumo wrestling contest, with power counting for far more than finesse.

'I watched glimpses of Wales in the 2003 World Cup and you could see what they were trying to do,' said Ruddock. 'Their play was not only very attractive but also highly effective. When I took over from Steve Hansen, I sat down with Scott Johnson [the Wales skills coach] and discussed that style of rugby, of which I was a fan. The game has changed: with defences being so organised, seeking contact merely slows your ball down. It makes sense to avoid that, especially from set-pieces where the 16 forwards are committed in one little block. Instead of seeking contact with back-row moves, I would rather go wider and look for space. Scott has been instrumental in the way we have played: people think it is totally off the cuff, but there are a number of pre-planned patterns. The good coaches evolve their players: when I started off, players were very much coach-driven, but they are now taking real ownership of certain areas. They have shown me that they are real leaders and that augurs well for the future. We have to hang on to Scott and Andrew Hore [the conditioning coach]: they are men of quality who have played key parts in our success, along with the defence coach Clive Griffiths.

'The way we have attacked is down to Scott, while Andrew has conditioned the players so that they are able to play with width and continuity for the whole 80 minutes of a match. Our defence has been magnificent, thanks to Clive; you only have to look back at the final minutes in France when we were defending our line to appreciate the work Clive has done with the players. Another important factor was the part played by the four regions: they are stakeholders in the national team and, as well as watching other teams in the Six Nations for us and making presentations to the squad, they gave us their total co-operation when we asked for players to be rested before internationals. We were able to spend two weeks together before the England match, unlike our opponents who had had a couple of days with Leeds Rhinos before returning to their clubs for a round of Premiership matches. England picked up another couple of injuries that weekend, and we cannot argue that one of the factors behind our victory against them was that they were without a number of key players. One of the reasons players in Ireland and Wales prefer to stay in their respective countries rather than accept offers from English clubs is that they know that by staying at home they will prolong their careers, playing well into their 30s, whereas in England, clubs expect players to earn their wages.'

Johnson was recruited by Graham Henry at the end of 2001. He had been the Australia A assistant coach that year, helping mastermind a 28–25 victory over Henry's Lions. 'He is innovative and full of ideas,' Henry said at the time. 'He can do a job for us.' As Johnson arrived, Henry left, but the Australian became Steve Hansen's right-hand man, telling anyone who cared to listen, as Wales were sliding on their way to a whitewash in the 2003 Six Nations, that the good times were about to roll. 'We will be dark horses in the World Cup,' he had predicted. 'By the time October comes around, there will be no one who will relish playing us.' Few believed him at the time, but that autumn New Zealand and England came to understand precisely what the Australian had meant.

It was against the All Blacks in the World Cup that Wales rediscovered their attacking relish, but was their performance that day a consequence of planning or was it an accident? Wales's first three group matches had been largely turgid affairs: there were flourishes in the opening game against Canada, when the centre Iestyn Harris provided the creative spark, but against Tonga, then Italy, Wales were more one-dimensional than expansive in their approach. Hansen, at the time, insisted that it was not what he wanted. 'The players are feeling the pressure because, if they do not qualify for the quarter-finals, it will be the end of us as a team,' he said, in between the Italy and New Zealand Tests. He introduced a number of new faces against the All Blacks and was perceived to be resting players ahead of the quarter-final against England the following week. When that notion was put to him three days before the game, he had said: 'If you think that, wait and see.'

'What we saw against New Zealand came about partly by accident and partly by design,' said Mark Taylor, a centre under Hansen, who played on the wing in the final game of the 2005 Six Nations against Ireland. 'We cracked it when Shane Williams sidestepped out of the way of five defenders and everyone exploded onto it. It clicked for us, and it was what the coaches had been working towards. Scott Johnson organises touch rugby sessions in training: we do not play in the traditional way towards the posts, but from one touchline to the other. It encourages you to look for space and improves your passing and handling skills.'

When Hansen announced his intention to leave at the end of the 2004 Six Nations, Johnson did not apply to become the next Wales coach. He received an offer to return home and join the Australia coach Eddie Jones's management team, but opted to work under Ruddock. 'I felt that I had not finished the job,' he said. 'We had started something under Steve and I was determined to carry it on. I will stay in Wales as long as I am wanted; I do not worry about contracts or stuff like that. I'm as Welsh as they come now, and what we are about is not building a quality rugby team, but a quality rugby country: that means putting a system in place which ensures that Wales is there or thereabouts consistently. Young players coming through the system are being given every chance to develop and we are establishing an excellent production line. Professionalism is not about money as much as attitude. We have only just started.'

After Wales had defeated Scotland in their fourth match of the 2005 campaign, having led 38–3 at half-time, Johnson told the players that he was far from satisfied. 'In one way, it was a good thing that Scotland came back at us in the second half because it gave me plenty to work on,' he said. 'It was a great win, but we could sit back and see that things could have been done better. When Rhys Williams intercepted the ball for our second try, he did not run at 100 mph – he should have been going flat out. There were other things in the first half that day that I was not happy about, which is good because there is no better time to be critical than after a victory.'

Wales's success was heralded as a rediscovery of the Welsh way of doing things, yet before the start of the 2004 Six Nations Championship, David Pickering, the chairman of the Welsh Rugby Union, reflecting on the World Cup which had finished three months before, said: 'This season's tournament will give the side that emerged in Australia the chance to develop and prove that the style they played with in the World Cup can point our way forward to a more fruitful age – the Welsh way recaptured.' Recaptured by a New Zealander and an Australian. 'I have always said that a team has got to represent its coaches and what they stand for,' said Johnson after the Grand Slam triumph. 'This is a working class people; I consider myself a working class boy, Mike Ruddock is a working class boy. You have got to represent what you stand for and this team epitomises that. There are not any stars here: they are a bunch of guys who have grown up a long way.'

But what is the Welsh way? In 1976 the final team which

clinched the Grand Slam against France had been made up from eight clubs: London Welsh, Cardiff, Bridgend, Llanelli, Pontypool, Swansea, Aberavon and Pontypridd, sides which had their own distinct playing styles. Pontypool had supplied the front row: Tony Faulkner, Bobby Windsor and Graham Price. It was a club renowned for the ferocity of its forward play under its coach Ray Prosser, not a man who could ever be accused of letting romantic ideals get the better of him. 'I don't want ball-handlers,' he once famously said. 'I want man-handlers.' Pooler were then regarded as exponents of the nine-man game, the outside-half only receiving the ball when the forwards and the scrum-half had become fed up with it, which was not very often. Prosser inspired fear in his players, no matter how old or experienced they were. Any over-indulgence, with the ball in hand, was met with a stern rebuke afterwards. Eddie Butler, the rugby correspondent of *The Observer*, who captained Pontypool and Wales in the 1980s, tells the story of when Pontypool played Cambridge University at Pontypool Park towards the end of the 1970s. Butler was then a student at Cambridge, and Prosser, anxious to sign him and not wanting to give Butler's mother, who was sitting in the stand that night, the right impression, ordered his players to behave with total propriety in the match: no punching, kicking, stamping or any of the many other dark arts. If a Cambridge University player killed the ball, so be it. It was totally unlike Prosser, but no player would dare defy him.

As the match went on and the students realised that they could get away with anything, they killed the ball with impunity. The match was reaching its conclusion when the veteran international Faulkner, exasperation turning to rage after Cambridge University had come over on the wrong side for the umpteenth time, gave the miscreant, in the parlance of the time, a slippering. Immediately after he had wiped his studs on the light blue hooped jersey, he remembered his coach's injunction and turned to the sideline to face his glaring coach with panic written all over his face, spluttering out, 'I'm sorry, Pross, but he had to have it.'

Pontypool's way was not exactly that of Wales, and nor was Aberavon's. They, too, produced forwards whose fists appeared to have been hewn from granite: the likes of Omri Jones, Billy Mainwaring, Morton Howells and John Richardson inspired fear in opponents. 'I remember playing at Aberavon once when I had given their scrum-half a good clout,' said the former Gloucester, England and Lions' prop, Mike Burton. 'Omri Jones, their flanker and a policeman to boot, caught me with one after a lineout and I collapsed to the ground in agony, knowing I had broken some ribs. As I lay there, Jones came up and asked if I was all right, grinding his studs into my outstretched palm as he did so. Gloucester, like Bath and Bristol, played most of the leading Welsh clubs in the 1970s and they hardened us up. Wales had 16 top clubs then and every game was physical: they would dish it out, but they would take it without complaint. I remember being in Pontypool's medical room having 12 stitches inserted into a head wound and one of their officials brought me in a pint of beer. The Welsh had hard forwards and fleet-footed backs, even so-called second-class clubs like Crumlin, Abercarn and Bargoed that I played against for Gloucester United. Wales were in front of everybody else in those days. Many clubs who faced a day out at Aberavon, Pontypool, Ebbw Vale or Neath found several of their players discovering urgent business appointments, muscle twinges and dead grandmothers needing burial.'

Cardiff, Llanelli and Swansea liked to believe they were more refined that their valleys' cousins, but they also had their enforcers. 'The Welsh way was winning,' said the former England captain John Scott, who joined Cardiff from Rosslyn Park in 1978. 'Teams were physical, competitive, cunning and resourceful. At Cardiff, we had to be able to play the game more than one way and we became successful in the 1980s when we developed a hard-nosed set of forwards to complement the skill and pace we had out wide. What struck me most when I arrived in Wales was just how competitive rugby was from the youngest age-group level up. The comprehensive schools all played each other and youngsters came into the club system well versed in the rudiments of the game. It meant that teams were able to change tactics during the course of a game and react to events, rather than rely on coaches. I came to Wales because I wanted to improve as a player: the club game in England was, in those days, nowhere near as competitive. I used to receive plenty of sledging because of my nationality and you just gave it back in kind. One of my first games was against Aberavon: I was putting myself about and received a few warnings. I was not going to be put off and continued to offend them. The retribution was not long in coming and a fist smashed into my face. After I got up from the ground, blood pouring from my mouth, I realised that my front teeth were missing. The referee was going mad, determined to find the culprit and send him off. I saw him, slinking off to the sidelines to receive treatment on his fist – my teeth were embedded in his knuckles. I liked Wales so much I stayed there.'

As the 1970s graduated into the 1980s, the increasing influence of television and its armchair audience gradually sandpapered the rougher edges off the Welsh game. Unions became increasingly reliant on income from television contracts and other commercial deals, and rugby consequently became less a game for players and more a sport for those who paid for it; but these newcomers blanched at the sight of players trading punches or indulging in uglier practices, horrified that such acts were tolerated. As P.G. Wodehouse's fictional buffoon Bertie Wooster put it: 'Rugby football is a game I can't claim absolutely to understand in all its niceties. I can follow the broad principles; I know that the main scheme is to work the ball down the field somehow and deposit it over the line at the other end, and that, in order to squelch this programme, each side is allowed to put in a certain amount of assault and battery and do things to its fellow man which, if done elsewhere, would result in fourteen days without the option, coupled with some strong remarks from the Bench.'

Burton again: 'What you have to remember about the 1960s and 1970s is that while players knew they were going to be on the receiving end, there was a code of conduct which everyone was expected to observe. There were lines you did not cross. One of the reasons Wales produced so many great forwards was that they did not let you get away with or from anything: they would always even up the score on the field. I remember playing Cardiff when I was a youngster: they had an array of hard men – John O'Shea, Howard Norris, John Hickey and Lyn Baxter to name a few. Norris had been a prop on the 1966 Lions tour Down Under, a giant with great craggy features. I was delving around in a ruck when I felt someone's fingers in my eyes. I stood up and smashed Norris across the face, not knowing whether he was the guilty party or not. He nearly collapsed in astonishment, and when we formed up for the next scrummage and there had been no retaliation, I quickly decided that Norris was very frightened and would be like a man walking on eggshells for the rest of the match. I did not notice him slip his right arm off his hooker as we went down and I ran into a clenched fist travelling speedily in the opposite direction. "You've hit me and I've hit you," he said after I had come to my senses, blood running down my nose.'

At the start of the 1985–86 season, the WRU adopted a zero-policy on acts of violence: any player sent off for an act of foul play would be banned from international rugby for the rest of the campaign: skulduggery had come to be highlighted on television replays and the Union felt itself under pressure to clean up the game. The policy backfired when one of Wales's leading forwards, the second row Robert Norster, threw a punch at his opposite number Steve Sutton during a match between Cardiff and South Wales Police that December and was sent off. He missed the subsequent Five Nations campaign, along with another miscreant, the Swansea number 8 Richard Moriarty, and, with the Union struggling to distinguish between acts committed in the heat of the moment and premeditated foul play, Welsh forward play began to lose its edge and traditionally strong clubs began to decline, a trend accelerated by the decline of the sport in state schools. As the 1990s dawned, other countries, including England, developed on more professional lines, putting in management systems at national and club level, having set up a league structure in 1987. Whereas the Wales team which had played Scotland in 1967 was represented by 11 clubs, the national coach Graham Henry was choosing his team at the end of the 1990s from four of five Welsh clubs. The very competitiveness of the domestic game which had underpinned the national side had been eroded to the point where it was hindering, rather than helping, success on the international field.

Several of the legends of the 1970s had been lost to the game on retirement after publishing their autobiographies. The hypocrisy of the amateur code was such that while coaching organisers were allowed to make a living from the game, anyone who received £50 for writing a newspaper column was barred from taking an active part in rugby union for life. The likes of Barry John, Gareth Edwards, Phil Bennett, Mervyn Davies and Gerald Davies only had an input through the media after writing their autobiographies as soon as they had stopped playing and, as the relative failure from 1980 was followed by years of humiliation following the tour to New Zealand in 1988, so the criticism by players from different eras began to grate on their successors. Ten days after Wales had won the 2005 Grand Slam, the WRU chief executive, David Moffett, called on the former internationals who had criticised that year's squad in the past to start handing out praise. Moffett had in mind those who had been part of the failures in the 1980s and 1990s, rather than the golden era generation, when he said: 'Perhaps the former players who have criticised the team, but who have never achieved what these players have, will now give them their dues.' However, it was not players from the past who had given Hansen a win-or-else warning before the final friendly international in the build-up to the 2003 World Cup, the tournament when Welshness reasserted itself, nor was it former international players from the 1980s and 1990s who had been responsible for administrative suicide in that period. It was the WRU, motivated in part by self-preservation, who had made one knee-jerk reaction after another, not the players. It was the Union, not a disaffected group of players which, by sacking Tony Gray as the national coach three months after his side had won a Triple Crown in 1988, had set the game on the slippery slope towards obscurity. It was the WRU not past players which turned Wales from a pioneering power into a country which reacted, with increasing desperation, to the example of others. It was the Union, not former players, which changed everything but itself in Welsh rugby's darkest hour. And it was two New Zealanders, Graham Henry and Steve Hansen, who, by sticking two fingers up to an administration that was unable, or unwilling, to see the pair's vision, and instead just getting on with things regardless, who paved the way for Ruddock to lift the cup of success to the lips of a parched nation. It was emphatically not the Welsh Rugby Union.

Moffett had not been part of the administrative muddle in the years of failure, bringing a desperately needed, hard-nosed commercial edge when he took office at the end of 2002, which made his churlish remark about former players all the more disappointing and incomprehensible; it was exactly the type of comment which would have been made by the straw-clutchers of the past, looking back rather than forward. What Ruddock, who phlegmatically accepts that sport is about opinion, and his coaching staff need to know is that, if the Grand Slam is followed by a period of mediocrity, they will not find themselves following in the footsteps of the previous two coaches who had taken Wales to the top of the championship table. Just as Gray was not allowed to build on his success, so Alan Davies found himself being shown the door just 12 months after landing the 1994 Five Nations. When Ruddock was appointed in the summer of 2004, he was handed a two-year contract which the Union was keen for him to extend after Wales had won their opening four championship matches in 2005.

'Mike Ruddock has been superb,' said the former Llanelli and Wales centre Ray Gravell, a Grand Slam winner in 1976 and 1978. 'I appreciate that Steve Hansen did a lot of the groundwork, but Mike has been the catalyst for our success. He has made the side distinctly Welsh, reminding the players of the game's rich heritage. I have never made comparisons with the 1970s because there is nothing to be gained in doing so. The players of 2005 made their own history, and they did it in style, making a nation proud.' The Welsh way to Gravell is simple: 'It starts up front because you need a firm base, and I feel Mike Ruddock has provided that. You need a good, athletic back row, which we have in Ryan Jones, Martyn Williams and Michael Owen. Behind the scrum, the Welsh way is about not being afraid to make mistakes, being prepared to live off your wits. When I played for Llanelli, Carwyn James was the coach: he told me I would only learn by making mistakes and he made me feel I was a better player than I actually was. Psychology plays a big part in sport, and Mike Ruddock appreciates that.

'When you look back to the 2003 World Cup, our performance against New Zealand was exceptional, but you always felt in the back of your mind that the All Blacks were in control. The quarter-final against England was different: we were the better side, but lost. I left the ground that night feeling proud and disappointed at the same time. We are playing in more of a Welsh way now because we are more clinical in our finishing and our defence is rock solid. We can dream again: the prospect of winning the World Cup in 2007 is realistic, all the more so when you consider how close we were to making the semi-finals in 2003. Success will not go to the players' heads because of the disappointments they suffered before tasting success. They will take the accolades and then get on with the future.'

The future is often to be found in the past. The success of the 1970s did not suddenly happen. Gerald Davies's first four international appearances, between 1966 and 1967, all ended in defeat; Barry John also had to wait until his fifth Test to savour victory in a Wales jersey; Gareth Edwards was on the winning side just twice in his first seven internationals. The Grand Slam side of 1971 did not materialise out of nothing, any more than its 1950 counterpart had: Wales had won one match in each of the 1948 and 1949 Five Nations campaigns. 'The success of the 1970s was rooted in the club system,' said Burton. 'It will take a few years to evaluate properly how regional rugby will pan out, although the WRU's idea of centrally contracting the leading players would, in my view, be a bad move. It would take the passion out of the Welsh game and should be resisted by the regions.

'In the 1970s, Wales had players who were the best in their positions in the world: Barry John, Gareth Edwards, Graham

WILL YOU STILL LOVE ME TOMORROW?

Price, Mervyn Davies . . . you can go on and on. That fellow Edwards: I was on the 1974 Lions tour to South Africa with him. Early on we played Eastern Province. Gareth told us before the match: "These South Africans are playing in the same colours as Canterbury, and we all know what they tried to do to the Lions in 1971. This lot will try and play it as rough. All I ask of you [the forwards] is to let me get the ball out to the boys [the backs]." You knew what he meant. At the first lineout, I was standing at the front, rather than my normal position of three back. The ball went to Gareth and he quickly passed it away; it had reached the hands of the inside-centre when one of the Eastern Province front rowers smacked into Gareth as he lay on the ground. The guy had shot through a gap at the front of the lineout, but I was ready for him a second time: he tried it on after the next lineout, and as he was about to race past me, I stuck out my arm: he rushed on to it neck first and appeared to go round and round like a Catherine wheel. I said something comforting to him as he left the field on a stretcher. Gareth said nothing; he did not condone nor did he condemn what I had done, he just carried on getting the ball to his boys.

'Wales's Grand Slam team in 2005 probably did not have one player who was the best in his position in the world, but they were only just starting out. It was not the time to judge them. There was a Welshness about their play, but I would not say that their style was Welsh. That will come when their play in the set-pieces improves, and there were signs in the final match against Ireland that Mike Ruddock is making an impact in that area. The props' foot positioning at the scrum improved over the course of the five matches and they drove a few lineouts at the Irish. The success in future years will depend on how Wales use their semi-professional club game. It should be the ideal vehicle to bring through developing players and I think Wales will come to dominate the Celtic League.'

Others were less sanguine. Professor David Smith, writing in the *Western Mail* one week after the Six Nations trophy had been paraded around the Millennium Stadium, condemned the regional model. 'In an older Wales, the first class rugby clubs reflected their surrounding society,' he said. 'In this changing Wales, that real identification will only be rediscovered by sustaining equivalence which will also serve to cradle and show the supporters back to themselves. It is not sentiment which bemoans the demise of Ebbw Vale, Bridgend, Pontypridd, Swansea and so nearly Neath, but the clear hard-headed understanding that only on such traditions and localities as that of Neath can a sure-footed future be based. We may already have the model we seek in Neath-Swansea Ospreys, who are building towards adjacent valleys; Llanelli have always been the Scarlets and for decades have marketed themselves as West Wales and all points north; the Dragons are a split personality, with a crowd as loyal to Newport as it is yearning for a new hatching. Cardiff Blues are a playing shambles and a cultural mess, neither proud capital club nor feisty valleys commandos; they are not real. We should scrap the Orwellian fantasy of the regions and, with four franchised and renamed clubs, pull together localities over sensitively allotted areas to support what we all need to stand up for, a game that is as democratically based as it is professionally run. Or kiss it all a long goodbye.'

Smith's contention – he had started his column by saying that Welsh rugby was facing a crisis – was that, unlike any other period in the game's history, success was being driven from the top down, not from the bottom up. The impetus had been started by Henry and Hansen who had been appalled by the shocking state of the Welsh game's infrastructure. 'No one can be really sure that this top-down managerial revolution, including organisational change, will be sustained by grass roots which are now as dodgy in some places as the Millennium Stadium turf on which we began this amazing Grand Slam campaign,' said Smith. 'The challenge is to root this team in ways that can allow both it and Welsh rugby to grow for decades to come. At the moment the real difficulties in the way of this ambition are being air-brushed out by hype and commercialised ballyhoo.' He pointed out that four pivotal players in the victory over Ireland, the try scorers, Gethin Jenkins and Kevin Morgan, the captain, Michael Owen, and the player who kicked the ball out of play to bring home the Grand Slam, Martyn Williams, were all products of the Pontypridd youth team, a town which no longer had a professional team to support following the demise of Celtic Warriors the year before. All four regions were based along the M4 corridor. Would the Valleys in years to come have heroes to identify with? 'Welsh rugby should now lift its hooded eyes from the bottom line of the ledger and contemplate how the vital connection between its grass roots and its international triumph can be secured,' he added.

Smith's voice was lost in the euphoric roar which greeted Wales's first Grand Slam for more than a generation. A week after the victory over Ireland, the Ospreys won the Celtic League, Wales had won the Under-21 Grand Slam and they had enjoyed success at other age-group levels. 'Wales played the best rugby in the Six Nations, but I am not convinced they were the best side,' said Scott. 'France looked a more complete package and should really have won a second consecutive Grand Slam: they would have had they taken their chances against Wales in the first half in Paris. It's good for European rugby that Wales have come back after being out of the limelight for so long. Whether it will last will depend on whether David Moffett and the WRU can knock some sense into the likes of Cardiff Blues. England have had a transitional year, which was always going to happen after a World Cup win, and they will be back. The Six Nations was becoming boring: Wales have breathed new life back into it, but the success needs to stimulate the grass roots because the strength of the Welsh game when I arrived in Cardiff more than 25 years ago, its clubs and its schools, has now become one of its weaknesses.'

The WRU finished the 2005 Six Nations by looking ahead to its 125th anniversary in the 2005–06 season. It was trying to persuade New Zealand to agree to an international on the first Saturday in November to mark the centenary of the first meeting between the countries – Wales's still disputed 3–0 success in 1905. New Zealand had marked the Union's centenary in the 1980–81 season by turning up on the first Saturday in November and condemning Wales to their then second ever heaviest home defeat. The WRU of 2005 was far less complacent than its precursor in 1980 had been. The game had changed more in those 25 years than it had in the first 100 and, finally, having been pushed to the brink of financial ruin, the WRU at last changed with it. Moffett was not brought in by the elected general committee because he was wanted, but because he was needed. Only if he and his executives retain effective control will Ruddock and his management team be able to build on their successful start; if Moffett fails, and the amateur corps starts reasserting itself, the old volatilities and inconsistencies will return. 'We are going to lose a match again,' said Gravell. 'The important thing to is keep the faith because we know what the management and players are capable of. We must not make the mistake that we did after 1988 and 1994. After what we have been through, we cannot afford to. We have something capable of lasting and we must make it work.'

If 1979 marked the end of Welsh rugby's last successful era, would 2005 mark the start of the next one? 'This is a very good

Welsh side and it can go on to become great,' wrote Gareth Edwards, the symbol of the 1970s, in the *Western Mail*. 'It takes a team of special qualities to win the Grand Slam, and I am sure that everyone who was part of the teams which reached that level in 1971, 1976 and 1978, would join me in saluting Mike Ruddock and his players for their incredible achievement. When we last won the Grand Slam, there was an arrogance about the WRU that prevented the game from building on success. They thought the tide would turn when things started to go wrong. Those in power today must not let that happen again.'

Whatever Henry and Hansen achieve with New Zealand, they will do well to match their feat in forcing change on arguably the most conservative union, along with Scotland, in world rugby. They stormed the ramparts, clearing the way for Ruddock to add his flourish. In the hype of the moment, the notion that Wales had suddenly rediscovered their Welshness, something which many claimed had been suppressed by Henry, Hansen and Johnson, became popular. 'Before the 2003 World Cup, I was invited to the Wales squad's base in the Vale of Glamorgan to talk to the players about aspects of Wales and Welshness,' said David Smith. 'Steve Hansen was concerned that the squad did not fully understand their history and heritage. When I arrived, a woman was talking about Welsh love spoons; when it came to my turn, I tried to relate what I felt were fairly funny stories and it seemed to go well. After the tournament had ended, I went back to the Vale for a conference and bumped into Scott Johnson. I congratulated him on the performances against New Zealand and England, when, I remarked, Wales had played with their traditional flair. "Those are the games we lost," he replied.'

Two years on, Wales played with the same élan that they had displayed against New Zealand and England, but they were stronger physically and mentally. The victory over England made them believe, in themselves as much as in each other. They showed Welsh traits: able to think their way out of trouble, exemplified by Stephen Jones's break from his own 22 in Paris; the way Henson stole a couple of yards before taking a penalty from his own half against Ireland; Stephen Jones's tackle on Girvan Dempsey at a crucial moment in the game against the Irish, which brought to mind the late outside-half John Bevan's covering tackle in the corner in Paris in 1975; the resilience of the Wales tight five; the opportunism of Shane Williams, Kevin Morgan and Rhys Williams; the quick-thinking of Dwayne Peel; the inspired reading of games by Michael Owen and Martyn Williams; the passion of Gareth Thomas; the classical outside centre play of Tom Shanklin; and the star quality, a hallmark of successful Wales teams, of Henson.

It was a game based on thought as much as skill, athleticism, presence and conditioning and the Grand Slam was, ultimately, Ruddock's triumph. He had had to wait for his chance, never having made any secret of his ambition. A master of preparation, he balanced work with relaxation. He trusted his players, acknowledging the discipline instilled by Hansen and allowing them to leave their hotel for a couple of nights during the week of the Ireland game to return home to their families. The squad reflected the character of their coach, playing with a smile. They broke the mouldy state of the international game in Europe, and it was interesting to see England, in their final two matches of the 2005 Six Nations against Italy and Scotland, looking to off-load in the tackle, having won the World Cup while revelling in contact.

'I said to Mike on Grand Slam night that the hard work would start now,' said Ruddock's selection adviser, Alun Donovan. 'He replied: "I think I'll take tomorrow off."'

He didn't.

The 27-Year Itch

Wales after the 1978 Grand Slam

1979

Won the Triple Crown for a record fourth consecutive season.
Clinched the Five Nations crown for the seventh time that decade.
John Dawes stood down as coach, succeeded by John Lloyd.

1980

Finished third in the championship, their worst finish since 1968.
Flanker Paul Ringer sent off in the 9–8 defeat at Twickenham.
Welsh Rugby Union's centenary starts with a 23–3 reverse to New
    Zealand in Cardiff.

1981

Wales slump to fourth in the table after defeats in Edinburgh and
    Paris.
Full-back J.P.R. Williams among seven players dropped after
    15–6 defeat in Scotland.
Wales end the year by beating Australia in Cardiff 18–13.

1982

Wales lose their 14-year unbeaten home championship record,

Scotland winning 32–18.

Finish joint bottom with France after losing three of their four matches.

John Lloyd resigns as coach, replaced by John Bevan.

1983

Wales miss the chance to win the title by losing 16–9 in Paris on the final weekend.

England secure 13–13 draw in Cardiff, their best result at the ground for 20 years.

Wales finish the year with jaw-shattering 24–6 defeat against Romania in Bucharest.

1984

Hooker Mike Watkins becomes only the fourth player to lead Wales on debut after home defeat to Scotland.

Wales lose both championship matches at home for the first time since 1963.

Australia romp to a record 28–9 victory in Cardiff and a number of stalwarts announce their retirements from international rugby.

1985

Ireland win at the Arms Park for the first time since 1967.

Fly-half Gareth Davies quits in disgust after selectors name A.N. Other at outside-half for the final match against England.

John Bevan resigns as coach because of ill-health. Tony Gray takes over.

1986

Wales miss key forwards Robert Norster and Richard Moriarty after WRU crackdown on foul play.

THE 27-YEAR ITCH

Paul Thorburn kicks record 70-yard penalty during the victory over Scotland in Cardiff.

Wales win three summer tour matches in Fiji, Tonga and Western Samoa.

1987

Wales ranked as European outsiders for the World Cup after losing three Five Nations matches.

Beat England in World Cup quarter-finals, but crash out to New Zealand in the semis 49–6.

Finish third in the tournament after edging out Australia 22–21.

1988

Win the Triple Crown and the championship for the first time since 1979.

Tony Gray sacked after two 50-point shockers in New Zealand that summer, replaced by John Ryan.

Wales slump at home to Romania 15–9 in December.

1989

Wales finish with their first wooden spoon since 1967.

First ever whitewash avoided after final day victory against England.

New Zealand win 34–9 in Cardiff in November.

GRAND SLAM!

1990

John Ryan resigns midway through the campaign after 34–6 defeat at Twickenham.

Ron Waldron takes over but can't prevent the dreaded whitewash.

Wales win two summer Tests in Namibia unconvincingly.

1991

Wales finish bottom of the Five Nations for an unprecedented third successive season.

Ron Waldron resigns because of ill-health after humiliating tour to Australia, losing to New South Wales 71–8 and the Wallabies 63–6.

Alan Davies appointed caretaker coach for the World Cup, but Wales fail to qualify for the knock-out stage, losing to Western Samoa and Australia.

1992

Alan Davies takes over from Waldron permanently.

Wales win their opening championship match in Dublin.

Fail to score against England for the first time since 1962.

1993

Wales beat England at home 10–9.

Wing Nigel Walker scores Wales's first try in Paris for a decade.

Finish bottom of the table for the fourth time in five years.

1994

Wales win the Five Nations Championship for the first time since 1988.

France are defeated in Cardiff for the first time since 1982, the year Wales last won both their championship matches in Cardiff.

THE 27-YEAR ITCH

Wales reach three figures for the first time in beating Portugal 102–11 in a World Cup qualifier in Lisbon.

1995

Alan Davies resigns as coach after Wales's second whitewash in five years.

Alex Evans heads a three-man coaching team in the World Cup in South Africa – Mike Ruddock is one of his assistants.

Wales fail to make the quarter-finals for the second World Cup running – Kevin Bowring takes over as Wales coach in the autumn.

1996

Wales avoid another whitewash in beating France 16–15 on the final weekend, but still finish bottom.

The victory over France ended a record eight consecutive championship reverses.

Wales suffer two Test defeats in Australia in the summer, 56–25 and 42–3.

1997

Wales start the campaign with their first win at Murrayfield since 1985.

They lose the next three matches but stay off the bottom on points difference.

Neil Jenkins and Scott Gibbs help the Lions to a series win in South Africa.

1998

Wales – playing their home matches at Wembley – crash to record defeats against England (60–26) and France (51–0).

Kevin Bowring resigns and Dennis John takes over as caretaker coach for the tour to Zimbabwe and South Africa – Wales lose by a record 96–13 to the Springboks.

Graham Henry takes over as coach in August – Wales take a 14–0 lead in his first match in charge against South Africa, before losing 28–20.

1999

Wales lose their opening two matches in the Five Nations to Scotland and Ireland, but win their final two – in France for the first time since 1975 and against England at Wembley.

Wales become the first European team to whitewash the Pumas in a Test series in Argentina, having trailed 23–0 during the first international.

World Cup successes over Argentina and Japan extended hosts Wales's winning run to ten internationals, their best since 1910, but they are knocked out of the World Cup in the quarter-finals by Australia in Cardiff.

2000

The Five Nations becomes Six – Wales win three matches but suffer heavy defeats against France and England.

'Grannygate' Affair sees Wales's Kiwis Shane Howarth and Brett Sinkinson banned from international rugby.

Henry suffers a further blow when fitness coach Steve Black resigns because of media pressure.

2001

Wales suffer another losing start to the Six Nations with England winning 44–15 in Cardiff.

Win successive internationals in France for the first time since 1957 with 43–35 triumph in Paris.

The year finishes on a low as Ireland win 36–6 in Cardiff in a rearranged championship game before Argentina wreck Iestyn Harris's debut, 30–16.

2002

Henry stands down after opening championship match ends in a 54–10 reverse in Dublin.

Steve Hansen takes over on a two-year contract and Wales come within inches of beating France in his first match.

Hansen rings the changes on the two-Test summer tour to South Africa, and Wales twice push the Springboks close.

2003

Wales open their championship campaign by losing to Italy for the first time.

Finish bottom of the table after first Six Nations whitewash. Hansen under pressure after Wales lose a tenth consecutive Test, but they qualify for the World Cup quarter-finals and return home to a hero's welcome after storming displays against New Zealand and England.

2004

Wales win their opening championship match for the first time since 1997, beating Scotland 23–10 in Cardiff.

Finish fourth in the championship after pushing France and England close.

Steve Hansen becomes the first Wales coach to see out his allotted term since John Dawes in 1979. Mike Ruddock takes over in May.

2005

Grand Slam.

MATCH STATISTICS 2005

	P	W	D	L	F	A	Tries	Pts
WALES	5	5	0	0	151	77	17	10
France	5	4	0	1	134	82	13	8
Ireland	5	3	0	2	126	101	12	6
England	5	2	0	3	121	77	16	4
Scotland	5	1	0	4	84	155	8	2
Italy	5	0	0	5	55	179	5	0

APPENDIX 2

MATCH ANALYSIS

WALES 11 ENGLAND 9
Millennium Stadium, Cardiff, 5 February 2005, Att. 72,500

G. Thomas (Toulouse), captain **15** J. Robinson (Sale), captain
H. Luscombe (Newport-Gwent Dragons) **14** M. Cueto (Sale)
T. Shanklin (Cardiff Blues) **13** M. Tait (Newcastle)
G. Henson (Neath-Swansea Ospreys) **12** J. Noon (Newcastle)
S. Williams (Neath-Swansea Ospreys) **11** J. Lewsey (Wasps)
S. Jones (Clermont Auvergne) **10** C. Hodgson (Sale)
D. Peel (Llanelli Scarlets) **9** M. Dawson (Wasps)
G. Jenkins (Cardiff Blues) **1** G. Rowntree (Leicester)
M. Davies (Gloucester) **2** S. Thompson (Northampton)
A. Jones (Neath-Swansea Ospreys) **3** J. White (Leicester)
B. Cockbain (Neath-Swansea Ospreys) **4** D. Grewcock (Bath)
R. Sidoli (Cardiff Blues) **5** B. Kay (Leicester)
D. Jones (Llanelli Scarlets) **6** C. Jones (Sale)
M. Williams (Cardiff Blues) **7** A. Hazell (Gloucester)
M. Owen (Newport-Gwent Dragons) **8** J. Worsley (Wasps)

Replacements
Wales: **17** J. Yapp (Cardiff Blues) for A. Jones, 79; **18** J. Thomas (Neath-Swansea Ospreys) for Cockbain, 79; **19** R. Jones (Neath-Swansea Ospreys) for D. Jones, 67; **20** G. Cooper (Newport-Gwent Dragons) for Peel, 64; **22** K. Morgan (Cardiff Blues) for Luscombe, 68
  Unused replacements: **16** R. McBryde (Llanelli Scarlets); **21** C. Sweeney (Newport-Gwent Dragons)

England: **17** P. Vickery (Gloucester) for Rowntree, 59; **18** S. Borthwick (Bath) for Grewcock, 71; **19** J. Forrester (Gloucester) for Worsley, 42–44; **20** H. Ellis (Leicester) for Dawson, 67; **21** O. Barkley (Bath) for Tait, 62
  Unused replacements: **16** A. Titterrell (Sale); **22** B. Cohen (Northampton)

Scorers: WALES – Try S. Williams; Penalties S. Jones, Henson
      ENGLAND – Penalties Hodgson 3

Referee: S. Walsh (New Zealand)

Official data & statistics partner of the
RBS 6 Nations Championship

THE RBS 6 NATIONS - CARDIFF MILLENNIUM - 05.02.05

WALES	ENGLAND
11	**9**
8	HT	3

Try	1	PenTry	0
Conversions		0 / 1	
Penalty Goals		2 / 4	
Drop Goals		0 / 2	

Phases of Play

Scrums Won	7
Lost	1
Lineouts Won	15
Lost	3
Pens Conceded	13
Freekick Conceded	0
Mauls Won	2
Ruck and Drive	25
Ruck and Pass	21

Ball Won

In Open Play	48
In Opponent's 22	21
At Set Pieces	32
Turnovers Won	6

Team Statistics

Passes Completed	99
Line Breaks	11
Possession Kicked	29
Errors from Kicks	8
Kicks to Touch	9
Kicks / Passes	22%
Tackles Made	66
Missed	8
Tackle Completion	89%
Offloads in Tackle	2
Offloads / Tackled	3%
Total Errors Made	19
Errors / Ball Won	23%

Minutes in Possession

1	13:44	2	15:33

Mins in Opponent's Half

1	26:49	2	27:32

S JONES - PenMiss	8:37
S WILLIAMS - Try	10:42
S JONES - ConMiss	11:50
HODGSON - Penalty	15:05
HODGSON - DropMiss	19:23
S JONES - DropMiss	21:14
S JONES - Penalty	24:51
GREWCOCK - Sin Bin	37:08
G THOMAS - Sin Bin	37:21
HODGSON - PenMiss	41:59
HT	
Forrester on for Worsley	1:31
Worsley on for Forrester	3:29
HODGSON - Penalty	9:13
Vickery on for Rowntree	18:38
S JONES - PenMiss	20:01
Barkley on for Tait	21:22
Cooper on for Peel	23:17
Ellis on for Dawson	26:10
R Jones on for D Jones	26:21
Morgan on for Luscombe	27:41
Borthwick on for Grewcock	30:32
HODGSON - Penalty	33:51
Rowntree on for White	37:13
Yapp on for A Jones	38:07
J Thomas on for Cockbain	38:32
HENSON - Penalty	41:21
HENSON - DropMiss	44:48

Try	0	PenTry	0
Conversions		0 / 0	
Penalty Goals		3 / 4	
Drop Goals		0 / 1	

Phases of Play

Scrums Won	8
Lost	0
Lineouts Won	17
Lost	3
Pens Conceded	10
Freekick Conceded	1
Mauls Won	9
Ruck and Drive	29
Ruck and Pass	17

Ball Won

In Open Play	55
In Opponent's 22	6
At Set Pieces	38
Turnovers Won	3

Team Statistics

Passes Completed	63
Line Breaks	16
Possession Kicked	26
Errors from Kicks	6
Kicks to Touch	13
Kicks / Passes	29%
Tackles Made	55
Missed	4
Tackle Completion	93%
Offloads in Tackle	4
Offloads / Tackled	6%
Total Errors Made	22
Errors / Ball Won	23%

Minutes in Possession

1	14:08	2	17:51

Mins in Opponent's Half

1	15:56	2	18:04

Top Carries	
Shanklin	5
Henson	4
S Williams	4
Robinson	3
D Jones	2

Top Tacklers	
M Williams	10
Kay	8
Hazell	7
Henson	7
S Jones	7

Most Missed Tackles	
Noon	3
Cockbain	2
A Jones	1
Davies	1
Henson	1

Most Off-Loads	
Cueto	1
Ellis	1
Kay	1
Lewsey	1
Luscombe	1

Most Errors	
Hodgson	4
S Jones	4
Dawson	3
Lewsey	3
Thompson	3

213

GRAND SLAM!

ITALY 8 WALES 38

Stadio Flaminio, Rome, 12 February 2005, Att. 25,659

R. de Marigny (Overmach Parma) **15** G. Thomas (Toulouse), captain
Mirco Bergamasco (Stade Français) **14** H. Luscombe (Newport-Gwent Dragons)
W. Pozzebon (Treviso) **13** T. Shanklin (Cardiff Blues)
A. Masi (Viadana) **12** G. Henson (Neath-Swansea Ospreys)
L. Nitoglia (Calvisano) **11** S. Williams (Neath-Swansea Ospreys)
L. Orquera (Padova) **10** S. Jones (Clermont Auvergne)
A. Troncon (Treviso) **9** D. Peel (Llanelli Scarlets)
A. Lo Cicero (L'Aquila) **1** G. Jenkins (Cardiff Blues)
F. Ongaro (Treviso) **2** M. Davies (Gloucester)
M. Castrogiovanni (Calvisano) **3** A. Jones (Neath-Swansea Ospreys)
S. Dellape (Agen) **4** B. Cockbain (Neath-Swansea Ospreys)
M. Bortolami (Narbonne), captain **5** R. Sidoli (Cardiff Blues)
A. Persico (Agen) **6** J. Thomas (Neath-Swansea Ospreys)
Mauro Bergamasco (Stade Français) **7** M. Williams (Cardiff Blues)
S. Parisse (Treviso) **8** M. Owen (Newport-Gwent Dragons)

Replacements
Italy: **16** S. Perugini (Calvisano) for Castrogiovanni, 61; **17** G. Intoppa (Calvisano) for Ongaro, 72; **18** C. del Fava (Rugby Parma) for Dellape, 61; **19** D. Dal Maso (Treviso) for Mauro Bergamasco, 29; **20** P. Griffen (Calvisano) for Troncon, 60; **21** M. Barbini (Padova) for Masi, 23–26 & for de Marigny, 80; **22** K. Robertson (Viadana) for Mirco Bergamasco, 56

Wales: **16** R. McBryde (Llanelli Scarlets) for Davies, 66; **17** J. Yapp (Cardiff Blues) for A. Jones, 66; **18** I. Gough (Newport-Gwent Dragons) for Cockbain, 66; **19** R. Sowden-Taylor (Cardiff Blues) for M. Williams, 80; **20** G. Cooper (Newport-Gwent Dragons) for Peel, 61; **21** C. Sweeney (Newport-Gwent Dragons) for S. Jones, 65; **22** K. Morgan (Cardiff Blues) for Luscombe, 57

Scorers: ITALY – Try Orquera; Penalty de Marigny
WALES –Tries J. Thomas, Shanklin, M. Williams, Cockbain,
S. Williams, Sidoli; Conversions S. Jones 4

Referee: A. Cole (Australia)

**Official data & statistics partner of the
RBS 6 Nations Championship**

THE RBS 6 NATIONS - ROME - 12.02.05

ITALY	WALES
8	**38**
5	HT	19

Italy				Time	Event	Wales			
Try	1	PenTry	0	4:13	J THOMAS - Try	Try	6	PenTry	0
Conversions		0 / 1		5:12	S JONES - Conversion	Conversions		4 / 6	
Penalty Goals		1 / 3		10:15		Penalty Goals		0 / 1	
Drop Goals		0 / 0	ORQUERA - Try			Drop Goals		0 / 0	
			DE MARIGNY - ConMiss	11:22					
				22:07	SHANKLIN - Try				
Phases of Play				23:17	S JONES - ConMiss	**Phases of Play**			
Scrums Won	7		Barbini on for Masi	23:27		Scrums Won	9		
Lost	0		Dal Maso on for M Bergamasco	25:47		Lost	0		
Lineouts Won	15		Masi on for Barbini	26:33		Lineouts Won	13		
Lost	3		DE MARIGNY - PenMiss	27:52		Lost	4		
Pens Conceded	5		DE MARIGNY - PenMiss	29:47		Pens Conceded	8		
Freekick Conceded	4			32:58	HENSON - PenMiss	Freekick Conceded	4		
Mauls Won	2			43:46	M WILLIAMS - Try	Mauls Won	3		
Ruck and Drive	35			44:31	S JONES - Conversion	Ruck and Drive	27		
Ruck and Pass	20			HT		Ruck and Pass	20		
			DE MARIGNY - Penalty	4:57					
Ball Won				15:09	COCKBAIN - Try	**Ball Won**			
In Open Play	57			15:51	S JONES - Conversion	In Open Play	50		
In Opponent's 22	10			16:14	Morgan on for Luscombe	In Opponent's 22	8		
At Set Pieces	30		Robertson on for Mi Bergamasco	16:45		At Set Pieces	27		
Turnovers Won	4			19:15	S WILLIAMS - Try	Turnovers Won	10		
				19:53	S JONES - Conversion				
Team Statistics				20:07	Cooper on for Peel	**Team Statistics**			
Passes Completed	97		Griffen on for Troncon	20:32		Passes Completed	136		
Line Breaks	7		Perugini on for Dellape	21:05		Line Breaks	14		
Possession Kicked	28		Del Fava on for Castrogiovanni	21:13		Possession Kicked	34		
Errors from Kicks	8			23:52	Sweeney on for S Jones	Errors from Kicks	14		
Kicks to Touch	6			25:31	Mcbryde on for Davies	Kicks to Touch	10		
Kicks / Passes	22%			25:36	Yapp on for A Jones	Kicks / Passes	20%		
				25:42	Gough on for Cockbain				
Tackles Made	79		Intoppa on for Ongaro	32:46		Tackles Made	71		
Missed	14			36:30	SIDOLI - Try	Missed	8		
Tackle Completion	84%			37:43	HENSON - ConMiss	Tackle Completion	89%		
			Barbini on for De Marigny	40:23					
Offloads in Tackle	10			40:48	Sowden-taylor on for M Williams	Offloads in Tackle	19		
Offloads / Tackled	14%					Offloads / Tackled	24%		
Total Errors Made	28					Total Errors Made	27		
Errors / Ball Won	32%					Errors / Ball Won	35%		

Minutes in Possession						**Minutes in Possession**			
1	09:52	2	18:03			1	16:52	2	14:14

Mins in Opponent's Half						**Mins in Opponent's Half**			
1	17:35	2	20:41			1	24:16	2	26:56

Top Carries		*Top Tacklers*		*Most Missed Tackles*		*Most Off-Loads*		*Most Errors*	
G Thomas	5	J Thomas	9	Orquera	3	G Thomas	2	Orquera	6
Henson	5	Persico	8	Masi	2	Henson	2	Henson	5
Nitoglia	5	Shanklin	8	Parisse	2	Luscombe	2	Masi	5
Parisse	5	Bortolami	7	Persico	2	Masi	2	G Thomas	3
S Williams	5	M Williams	7	Bortolami	1	Nitoglia	2	Peel	3

215

GRAND SLAM!

FRANCE 18 WALES 24

Stade de France, Paris, 26 February 2005, Att. 78,250

J. Laharrague (Brive) **15** G. Thomas (Toulouse), captain
A. Rougerie (Clermont Auvergne) **14** K. Morgan (Newport-Gwent Dragons)
D. Traille (Biarritz) **13** T. Shanklin (Cardiff Blues)
Y. Jauzion (Toulouse) **12** G. Henson (Neath-Swansea Ospreys)
C. Dominici (Stade Francais) **11** S. Williams (Neath-Swansea Ospreys)
Y. Delaigue (Castres) **10** S. Jones (Toulouse)
D. Yachvili (Biarritz) **9** D. Peel (Llanelli Scarlets)
S. Marconnet (Stade Français) **1** G. Jenkins (Cardiff Blues)
S. Bruno (Toulouse) **2** M. Davies (Gloucester)
N. Mas (Perpignan) **3** A. Jones (Neath-Swansea Ospreys)
F. Pelous (Toulouse), captain **4** B. Cockbain (Neath-Swansea Ospreys)
J. Thion (Biarritz) **5** R. Sidoli (Cardiff Blues)
S. Betsen (Biarritz) **6** R. Jones (Neath-Swansea Ospreys)
N. Nyanga (Béziers) **7** M. Williams (Cardiff Blues)
J. Bonnaire (Bourgoin) **8** M. Owen (Newport-Gwent Dragons)

Replacements
France: **16** W. Servat (Toulouse) for Bruno, 41; **17** O. Milloud (Bourgoin) for
Mas, 52; **18** G. Lamboley (Toulouse) for Thion, 74; **19** I. Harinordoquy
(Biarritz) for Bonnaire, 60; **21** F. Michalak (Toulouse) for Delaigue, 52;
22 J-P. Grandclaude (Perpignan) for Traille, 46
   Unused replacement: **20** P. Mignoni (Clermont Auvergne)

Wales: **16** R. McBryde (Llanelli Scarlets) for Davies, 65; **17** J. Yapp (Cardiff
Blues) for A. Jones, 67; **18** J. Thomas (Neath-Swansea Ospreys) for R. Jones,
77; **20** G. Cooper (Newport-Gwent Dragons) for Peel, 67; **21** C. Sweeney
(Newport-Gwent Dragons) for K. Morgan, 52–60; **22** R. Williams (Cardiff
Blues) for G. Thomas, 40
   Unused replacement: **19** R. Sowden-Taylor (Cardiff Blues)

Scorers: FRANCE – Tries Yachvili, Rougerie; Conversion Yachvili;
Penalty Yachvili; Drop goal Michalak
WALES – Tries M. Williams 2; Conversion S. Jones;
Penalties S. Jones 3; Drop goal S. Jones

Referee: P. Honiss (New Zealand)

THE RBS 6 NATIONS - STADE DE FRANCE - 26.02.05

FRANCE	WALES
18	**24**
15	HT	6

FRANCE

Try	2	PenTry	0
Conversions		1 / 2	
Penalty Goals		1 / 1	
Drop Goals		1 / 2	

Phases of Play
Scrums Won	12
Lost	0
Lineouts Won	17
Lost	3
Pens Conceded	9
Freekick Conceded	3
Mauls Won	5
Ruck and Drive	28
Ruck and Pass	36

Ball Won
In Open Play	69
In Opponent's 22	35
At Set Pieces	34
Turnovers Won	8

Team Statistics
Passes Completed	164
Line Breaks	15
Possession Kicked	22
Errors from Kicks	5
Kicks to Touch	10
Kicks / Passes	11%
Tackles Made	75
Missed	6
Tackle Completion	92%
Offloads in Tackle	18
Offloads / Tackled	20%
Total Errors Made	31
Errors / Ball Won	30%

Minutes in Possession
1	13:38	2	14:10

Mins in Opponent's Half
1	30:25	2	23:02

Match Events

FRANCE	Time	WALES
YACHVILI - Try	3:30	
YACHVILI - Conversion	4:31	
ROUGERIE - Try	13:13	
YACHVILI - ConMiss	14:00	
TRAILLE - DropMiss	18:28	
	25:00	S JONES - Penalty
YACHVILI - Penalty	27:38	
	44:02	S JONES - Penalty
	HT	
Servat on for Bruno		
		R Williams on for G Thomas
	1:04	M WILLIAMS - Try
	1:43	S JONES - Conversion
	4:50	M WILLIAMS - Try
Grandclaude on for Traille	6:12	
	6:29	S JONES - ConMiss
Milloud on for Mas	9:06	
Michalak on for Delaigue	11:16	
	12:33	Sweeney on for Morgan
	15:19	HENSON - PenMiss
Harinordoquy on for Bonnaire	20:22	
	20:35	Morgan on for Sweeney
MICHALAK - Drop Goal	24:48	
	25:23	Mcbryde on for Davies
	27:53	S JONES - Penalty
	28:02	Yapp on for A Jones
	28:13	Cooper on for Peel
	34:02	S JONES - Drop Goal
Lamboley on for Thion	35:38	
	40:11	J Thomas on for R Jones

WALES

Try	2	PenTry	0
Conversions		1 / 2	
Penalty Goals		3 / 4	
Drop Goals		1 / 1	

Phases of Play
Scrums Won	11
Lost	0
Lineouts Won	15
Lost	4
Pens Conceded	5
Freekick Conceded	1
Mauls Won	3
Ruck and Drive	33
Ruck and Pass	22

Ball Won
In Open Play	58
In Opponent's 22	9
At Set Pieces	35
Turnovers Won	9

Team Statistics
Passes Completed	112
Line Breaks	10
Possession Kicked	30
Errors from Kicks	7
Kicks to Touch	11
Kicks / Passes	21%
Tackles Made	88
Missed	12
Tackle Completion	88%
Offloads in Tackle	18
Offloads / Tackled	24%
Total Errors Made	26
Errors / Ball Won	27%

Minutes in Possession
1	11:22	2	10:47

Mins in Opponent's Half
1	12:26	2	22:11

Top Carries
Rougerie	7
Iaharrague	6
Traille	4
Delaigue	3
S Williams	3

Top Tacklers
M Williams	12
S Jones	12
Thion	10
Betsen	9
Henson	8

Most Missed Tackles
S Jones	2
Shanklin	2
A Jones	1
Betsen	1
Bonnaire	1

Most Off-Loads
Betsen	3
Michalak	3
Nyanga	3
Peel	3
Rougerie	3

Most Errors
Iaharrague	5
Rougerie	5
Davies	4
S Jones	4
Bruno	3

GRAND SLAM!

SCOTLAND 22 WALES 46

Murrayfield, Edinburgh, 13 March 2005, Att. 63,431

C. Paterson (Edinburgh) **15** K. Morgan (Newport-Gwent Dragons)
R. Lamont (Glasgow) **14** R. Williams (Cardiff Blues)
A. Craig (Glasgow) **13** T. Shanklin (Cardiff Blues)
H. Southwell (Edinburgh) **12** G. Henson (Neath-Swansea Ospreys)
S. Lamont (Glasgow)) **11** S. Williams (Neath-Swansea Ospreys)
D. Parks (Glasgow) **10** S. Jones (Clermont Auvergne)
C. Cusiter (Borders) **9** D. Peel (Llanelli Scarlets)
T. Smith (Northampton) **1** G. Jenkins (Cardiff Blues)
G. Bulloch (Glasgow), captain **2** M. Davies (Gloucester)
G. Kerr (Leeds) **3** A. Jones (Neath-Swansea Ospreys)
S. Grimes (Newcastle) **4** B. Cockbain (Neath-Swansea Ospreys)
S. Murray (Edinburgh) **5** R. Sidoli (Cardiff Blues)
S. Taylor (Edinburgh) **6** R. Jones (Neath-Swansea Ospreys)
J. Petrie (Glasgow) **7** M. Williams (Cardiff Blues)
A. Hogg (Edinburgh) **8** M. Owen (Newport-Gwent Dragons), captain

Replacements

Scotland: **17** B. Douglas (Borders) for Kerr, h-t; **18** N. Hines (Edinburgh) for Grimes, h-t; **20** M. Blair (Edinburgh) for Cusiter, 44; **21** G. Ross (Leeds) for Parks, h-t; **22** A. Henderson (Glasgow) for Craig, 76
    Unused replacements: **16** R. Russell (London Irish); **19** J. Dunbar (Leeds)

Wales: **16** R. McBryde (Lanelli Scarlets) for Davies, 48; **17** J. Yapp (Cardiff Blues) for A. Jones, 63; **18** J. Thomas (Neath-Swansea Ospreys) for Cockbain, 70; **21** C. Sweeney (Newport-Gwent Dragons) for Henson 75; **22** H. Luscombe (Newport-Gwent Dragons) for Shanklin, 8–16 & for R. Williams, 68
    Unused replacements: **19** R. Sowden-Taylor (Cardiff Blues); **20** M. Phillips (Llanelli Scarlets)

Scorers: SCOTLAND – Tries Craig, R. Lamont, Paterson;
Conversions Paterson 2; Penalty Paterson
WALES – Tries R. Jones, R. Williams 2, S. Williams, Morgan 2;
Conversions S. Jones 5; Penalties S. Jones 2

Referee: J. Kaplan (South Africa)

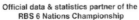

Official data & statistics partner of the
RBS 6 Nations Championship

THE RBS 6 NATIONS - MURRAYFIELD - 13.03.05

SCOTLAND	WALES
22	**46**
3	HT	38

SCOTLAND			Time	Event	WALES		
Try	3	PenTry 0	3:15	R JONES - Try	Try	6	PenTry 0
Conversions	2 / 3		4:11	S JONES - Conversion	Conversions	5 / 6	
Penalty Goals	1 / 1		7:35	Luscombe on for Shanklin	Penalty Goals	2 / 2	
Drop Goals	0 / 0		9:56	R WILLIAMS - Try	Drop Goals	0 / 0	
			10:42	S JONES - Conversion			
Phases of Play			13:54	S WILLIAMS - Try	**Phases of Play**		
Scrums Won	14		14:21	S JONES - Conversion	Scrums Won	9	
Lost	0		15:43	Luscombe on for Shanklin	Lost	0	
Lineouts Won	12		18:59	S JONES - Penalty	Lineouts Won	17	
Lost	2	PATERSON - Penalty	23:31		Lost	1	
Pens Conceded	8		28:00	MORGAN - Try	Pens Conceded	10	
Freekick Conceded	1		28:33	S JONES - Conversion	Freekick Conceded	0	
Mauls Won	3		42:34	MORGAN - Try	Mauls Won	3	
Ruck and Drive	46		43:03	S JONES - Conversion	Ruck and Drive	13	
Ruck and Pass	74		HT		Ruck and Pass	62	
		Douglas on for Kerr	0:03				
Ball Won		Hines on for Grimes	0:11		**Ball Won**		
In Open Play	123	Ross on for Parks	0:17		In Open Play	78	
In Opponent's 22	77	Blair on for Cusiter	4:40		In Opponent's 22	18	
At Set Pieces	36		9:21	R WILLIAMS - Try	At Set Pieces	34	
Turnovers Won	9		10:02	Mcbryde on for Davies	Turnovers Won	10	
			10:13	S JONES - ConMiss			
Team Statistics		CRAIG - Try	13:54		**Team Statistics**		
Passes Completed	214	PATERSON - Conversion	14:37		Passes Completed	201	
Line Breaks	7		21:57	COCKBAIN - Sin Bin	Line Breaks	9	
Possession Kicked	19		26:29	Yapp on for A Jones	Possession Kicked	17	
Errors from Kicks	3	R LAMONT - Try	30:31		Errors from Kicks	3	
Kicks to Touch	10	PATERSON - ConMiss	31:30		Kicks to Touch	7	
Kicks / Passes	8%		31:59	Luscombe on for R Williams	Kicks / Passes	7%	
		PATERSON - Try	33:30				
Tackles Made	122		33:40	Thomas on for Cockbain	Tackles Made	160	
Missed	14	PATERSON - Conversion	34:08		Missed	25	
Tackle Completion	89%		37:46	S JONES - Penalty	Tackle Completion	86%	
			38:36	Sweeney on for Henson			
Offloads in Tackle	15	Henderson on for Craig	38:55		Offloads in Tackle	19	
Offloads / Tackled	9%				Offloads / Tackled	15%	
Total Errors Made	22				Total Errors Made	24	
Errors / Ball Won	13%				Errors / Ball Won	21%	

Minutes in Possession			**Minutes in Possession**		
1	15:39	2 20:57	1	20:00	2 13:24

Mins in Opponent's Half			**Mins in Opponent's Half**		
1	18:08	2 30:00	1	29:32	2 15:36

Top Carries		Top Tacklers		Most Missed Tackles		Most Off-Loads		Most Errors	
S Lamont	13	R Jones	18	M Williams	5	Henson	3	Paterson	5
Paterson	12	Henson	16	Southwell	4	S Lamont	3	Davies	4
Taylor	12	Davies	13	Cockbain	3	Blair	2	Bulloch	3
R Jones	11	Petrie	13	Jenkins	3	Cockbain	2	Hogg	3
S Williams	10	M Williams	11	Bulloch	2	Hines	2	S Jones	3

GRAND SLAM!

WALES 32 IRELAND 20

Millennium Stadium, Cardiff, 19 March 2005, Att. 74,000

K. Morgan (Newport-Gwent Dragons) **15** G. Murphy (Leicester)
R. Williams (Cardiff Blues) **14** G. Dempsey (Leinster)
T. Shanklin (Cardiff Blues) **13** B. O'Driscoll (Leinster), captain
G. Henson (Neath-Swansea Ospreys) **12** K. Maggs (Ulster)
S. Williams (Neath-Swansea Ospreys) **11** D. Hickie (Leinster)
S. Jones (Clermont Auvergne) **10** R. O'Gara (Munster)
D. Peel (Llanelli Scarlets) **9** P. Stringer (Munster)
G. Jenkins (Cardiff Blues) **1** R. Corrigan (Leinster)
M. Davies (Gloucester) **2** S. Byrne (Leinster)
A. Jones (Neath-Swansea Ospreys) **3** J. Hayes (Munster)
B. Cockbain (Neath-Swansea Ospreys) **4** M. O'Kelly (Leinster)
R. Sidoli (Cardiff Blues) **5** P. O'Connell (Munster)
R. Jones (Neath-Swansea Ospreys) **6** S. Easterby (Llanelli Scarlets)
M. Williams (Cardiff Blues) **7** J. O'Connor (Wasps)
M. Owen (Newport-Gwent Dragons), captain **8** A. Foley (Munster)

Replacements
Wales: **16** R. McBryde (Llanelli Scarlets) for Davies, 72; **17** J. Yapp (Cardiff Blues) for A. Jones, 70
Unused replacements: **18** J. Thomas (Neath-Swansea Ospreys); **19** R. Sowden-Taylor (Cardiff Blues); **20** M. Phillips (Llanelli Scarlets); **21** C. Sweeney (Newport-Gwent Dragons); **22** H. Luscombe (Newport-Gwent Dragons)

Ireland: **16** F. Sheahan (Munster) for Byrne, 65; **17** M. Horan (Munster) for Corrigan, 61; **18** D. O'Callaghan (Munster) for O'Kelly, 65; **19** E. Miller (Leinster) for Foley, 61; **21** D. Humphreys (Ulster) for O'Gara, 51
Unused replacements: **20** G. Easterby (Leinster); **22** G. Duffy (Harlequins)

Scorers: WALES – Tries Jenkins, Morgan; Conversions S. Jones 2;
Penalties Henson, S. Jones 4; Drop goal Henson
IRELAND – Tries Horan, Murphy; Conversions Humphreys 2;
Penalties O'Gara 2

Referee: C. White (England)

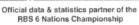

Official data & statistics partner of the
RBS 6 Nations Championship

THE RBS 6 NATIONS - CARDIFF MILLENNIUM - 19.03.05

WALES	IRELAND
32	**20**
16	HT	6

Try	2	PenTry	0
Conversions		2 / 2	
Penalty Goals		5 / 6	
Drop Goals		1 / 1	

Phases of Play

Scrums Won	9
Lost	0
Lineouts Won	13
Lost	4
Pens Conceded	10
Freekick Conceded	1
Mauls Won	0
Ruck and Drive	28
Ruck and Pass	17

Ball Won

In Open Play	45
In Opponent's 22	11
At Set Pieces	33
Turnovers Won	10

Team Statistics

Passes Completed	84
Line Breaks	14
Possession Kicked	27
Errors from Kicks	7
Kicks to Touch	9
Kicks / Passes	24%
Tackles Made	91
Missed	9
Tackle Completion	91%
Offloads in Tackle	8
Offloads / Tackled	14%
Total Errors Made	19
Errors / Ball Won	24%

Minutes in Possession

1	10:39	2	10:46

Mins in Opponent's Half

1	22:22	2	13:15

	S JONES - PenMiss
2:42	O'GARA - Penalty
5:33	HENSON - Drop Goal
12:37	JENKINS - Try
16:16	S JONES - Conversion
17:23	HENSON - Penalty
23:50	S JONES - Penalty
32:28	
36:27	O'GARA - Penalty
HT	
2:51	S JONES - Penalty
6:40	O'GARA - PenMiss
10:48	S JONES - Penalty
10:56	Humphreys on for O'gara
20:05	MORGAN - Try
21:10	S JONES - Conversion
21:54	Miller on for Foley
22:02	Horan on for Corrigan
25:16	Sheahan on for Byrne
25:27	O'Callaghan on for O'Kelly
28:41	HORAN - Try
29:10	HUMPHREYS - Conversion
29:26	Yapp on for A Jones
31:43	Mcbryde on for Davies
33:58	S JONES - Penalty
36:37	MURPHY - Try
37:36	HUMPHREYS - Conversion

Try	2	PenTry	0
Conversions		2 / 2	
Penalty Goals		2 / 3	
Drop Goals		0 / 0	

Phases of Play

Scrums Won	11
Lost	1
Lineouts Won	16
Lost	2
Pens Conceded	11
Freekick Conceded	0
Mauls Won	1
Ruck and Drive	41
Ruck and Pass	23

Ball Won

In Open Play	65
In Opponent's 22	23
At Set Pieces	37
Turnovers Won	2

Team Statistics

Passes Completed	109
Line Breaks	9
Possession Kicked	22
Errors from Kicks	8
Kicks to Touch	8
Kicks / Passes	16%
Tackles Made	57
Missed	7
Tackle Completion	89%
Offloads in Tackle	14
Offloads / Tackled	15%
Total Errors Made	21
Errors / Ball Won	20%

Minutes in Possession

1	10:14	2	14:20

Mins in Opponent's Half

1	22:36	2	31:56

Top Carries		Top Tacklers		Most Missed Tackles		Most Off-Loads		Most Errors	
Shanklin	6	M Williams	14	Jenkins	2	Hickie	3	S Jones	6
Murphy	5	S Jones	12	O'Gara	2	O'Driscoll	3	O'Gara	5
O'Driscoll	5	O'Connell	11	S Jones	2	Murphy	2	Davies	4
Peel	5	Shanklin	10	Henson	1	Owen	2	Dempsey	3
Foley	4	Henson	8	Hickie	1	Peel	2	Murphy	3

SUMMARY OF SCORING BY COUNTRY

TRIES

	For	Against
Wales	17	8
England	16	6
France	13	6
Ireland	12	9
Scotland	8	20
Italy	5	22

LEADING INDIVIDUAL SCORERS

Overall points

60 – Ronan O'Gara (Ireland)

57 – Stephen Jones (Wales)

53 – Dimitri Yachvili (France)

49 – Chris Paterson (Scotland)

37 – Charlie Hodgson (England)

20 – Mark Cueto (England)

17 – Roland De Marigny (Italy)

LEADING TRY SCORERS

4 – Mark Cueto (England)

3 – Martyn Williams, Shane Williams, Kevin Morgan (all Wales); Jamie Noon (England)

2 – Rhys Williams (Wales); Christophe Dominici, David Marty (both France); Geordan Murphy, Denis Hickie, Brian O'Driscoll (all Ireland); Josh Lewsey (England); Andy Craig (Scotland)

APPENDIX 3

MOST CONVERSIONS
12 – Stephen Jones (Wales)

MOST PENALTIES
12 – Ronan O'Gara (Ireland); Chris Paterson (Scotland)
10 – Stephen Jones (Wales)

MOST DROP GOALS
4 – Ronan O'Gara (Ireland)

APPENDIX 4

INTERNATIONAL RUGBY BOARD WORLD RANKINGS (APRIL 2005)

RANK	COUNTRY	RATING
1	New Zealand	90.90
2	Australia	88.58
3	South Africa	85.78
4	France	84.67
5	Wales	83.08
6	England	82.81
7	Ireland	82.14
8	Argentina	77.63
9	Fiji	74.17
10	Scotland	73.48